THE TALL AMERICAN

THE TALL AMERICAN

The Story of Gary Cooper

by RICHARD GEHMAN

ILLUSTRATED BY ALBERT MICALE

WITH TITLE PAGE ILLUSTRATION BY MARIA COOPER

Hawthorn Books, Inc.   *Publishers*   *New York*

To the memory of my good friend

JERRY WALD

CONTENTS

CHAPTER 1

THE BIG DECISION

Judge Charles Cooper was sitting in his study, surrounded by shelves of lawbooks, reading the evening paper, when his younger son, Frank, later to be known all over the world as Gary, knocked hesitantly.

"Could you give me a few minutes of your time, Father?" Frank Cooper asked.

"Certainly, my lad," the Judge said. He put down his newspaper as the young man came into the room. It is conceivable that he looked at him with approval. Frank Cooper was twenty-three, a gangly, not en-

9

tirely graceful fellow who stood six feet, three inches tall. His skin was deeply tanned, setting off his startlingly bright blue eyes. He looked as though he might be able to ride a horse well, which was in fact the case. He had grown up on the plains of Montana and virtually had spent his boyhood in the saddle.

Judge Cooper was an English immigrant who had come to the United States in 1885 with a pioneer's determination to make something of himself. He had held a variety of odd jobs while studying law, and eventually had been admitted to the bar. His diligence and integrity had won the respect of his neighbors in that rough country, and after some years they had honored him by giving him a seat on the bench of the Montana State Supreme Court. But now—this was the summer of 1924—Judge Cooper was temporarily living in Los Angeles. He had resigned from the bench to return to private practice, for a judge's salary had not been sufficient to permit him to support his wife and two sons. An estate case he was handling, a long and complicated legal matter, had brought him to California. He was biding his time until he could finish the job and get back to his beloved Montana.

Frank Cooper at the time was about to go into his third year at Grinnell College, Grinnell, Iowa. He was home for summer vacation, and he was working at whatever odd jobs he could find. He was uncertain as to what the future would hold for him, although his ambition at the time was to be an artist.

"Father, I've got an important decision to make," young Cooper said to the Judge. "I want your advice. What happened to me today may change my whole life."

"Oh, come, lad," said the Judge. "Surely you're joking. Sit down."

Frank Cooper lowered his towering frame into a chair opposite his father's.

"I met some fellows from Montana this morning," he said. "Some cowboys we used to know. They were on their way to a movie studio to get jobs. I went along with them. The man picked me for a job . . ." He paused, as though embarrassed.

"Well, well, that must have been a lark," the Judge said. "Did you actually appear in this cinema, Frank?"

"All I did was ride a horse," Frank said. He reached into his pocket and pulled something out. "Look at this." He was holding a ten-dollar bill.

The father stared in amazement. "You don't mean the people *paid* you all that just for riding a horse?"

Frank Cooper nodded, solemnly. "Yes, sir, they did. And, furthermore, Father, they want me to come back and do it again tomorrow."

The Judge frowned. "But what about your other job?"

"I'm really not doing very well at anything," the son said. "Everything I try seems . . . well, so futile."

"You've done very well, son," the Judge said. "You've worked your way through college so far, and you've never asked for a penny."

"I feel as though I ought to be doing more," said Frank Cooper, his face intensely serious. "And so, with your permission, sir, I've made up my mind. I've decided that I'm going to try to be a film actor."

If the Judge had been amazed before at the sight of the ten-dollar bill, he now was thunderstruck. For a moment he could not speak. Then he said, quietly, "Surely you can't be serious."

"I am, sir."

"You wish to be . . . *an actor?*"

"If I can. I don't know if I can. After all, I couldn't make the dramatic club in college. But this movie acting is different. I can play a cowboy, the men at the studio told me. All I have to do is ride and rope and shoot."

Carefully, the experienced lawyer and judge began to marshal evidence against what seemed to him a harebrained notion. He had hoped that his son would be a lawyer—or, at least, that he would graduate from college.

"The law is not for me," Frank Cooper said. "My

mind just isn't organized for the law, Father. And as for college . . . well, I'm getting along well enough there, but it seems foolishness to continue if I've got no goal in mind."

The Judge tried another tack. Film acting was not respectable, he declared.

"But it can be, sir. Right there today I met some fine fellows, just as fine as the cowboys back home. In fact, as I told you, some of them *were* cowpokes from back home. That's how I happened to go to the studio."

"But . . . could you earn a living at this trade?"

"There is a star named Tom Mix. I hear he earns five thousand dollars a week."

"I don't believe it."

"I'm sure it's true. Mix has a saddle trimmed with silver and gold. He rides around in a white limousine with a great big pair of a steer's longhorns as a radiator ornament. He is a millionaire many times over, Father."

The Judge was silent again for a time. "I had hoped you might go into something more worthwhile," he said.

The boy spoke softly, but his voice was resolute. "It seems to me that providing entertainment for hundreds of thousands of people could be worthwhile."

"You will get mixed up with the wrong sort of people, I fear."

"Father, isn't that more or less up to me? I've always been careful of my associations."

The two of them argued half the night. It was nearly three o'clock in the morning before they came to an agreement. Years later, Mrs. Alice Cooper, Gary's mother, recalled the scene vividly. "They were not angry," she said, "for they were both decent men. Father wanted the best for his son . . . but my boy was always determined. This time he was more determined than usual, and his father recognized that." The scene ended as follows:

"Very well, Frank," said the father. "I see that your mind is made up. I will give my permission in this way. You may try your acting career, if a career it indeed can be called, for one year. If, at the end of that time, you are not successful, you will return to college."

"It sometimes takes actors longer than a year to make good," Frank Cooper protested.

"One year," the father repeated.

"Very well. One year."

The exact date on which this discussion took place is impossible to determine; all that can be said is that the acting career of the young man began some time late in that summer of 1924. It lasted nearly four decades—until Saturday, May 13, 1961, when this valiant man succumbed to cancer and died with a priest at his side in his home in Hollywood.

During those years—thirty-seven of them—The Tall American (a nickname bestowed upon him by his friend Jerry Wald, the producer) carried out the aim he had set for himself in that original conversation with his father. Indeed, he did more. Instead of providing entertainment for hundreds of thousands, he brought pleasure—and, yes, inspiration—to millions, not only in the country in which he was born but in all the remote areas of the world where a motion picture projector could be set up and operated. Everywhere he was loved, everywhere admired. His face was as familiar to the fierce tribesmen of Afghanistan, who saw it on the screen of the dingy little theatre in Kabul, as it was to the people of New York City, of London and Paris and Hong Kong and Manila and Tokyo. To these people Gary Cooper was an actor, but he was also much, much more. They regarded him as an old and beloved friend. Crowds clustered around him wherever he went—in Berlin, in New Orleans, in Ankara. He could not walk down the street in any metropolis without attracting a huge retinue of adoring—but always respectful—admirers.

The magnetism, the dignity, and the air of simple,

solid friendliness and honesty that Gary Cooper carried with him attracted not only common folk but leaders of the world in all fields. He was the friend of Presidents and Prime Ministers, and of giants of the arts such as Pablo Picasso and Ernest Hemingway. He and his family visited Picasso in France, and David Douglas Duncan, the photographer, took a picture of the artist looking over some sketches by Cooper's daughter. Later, when Picasso was asked to sign the picture, he decided there was too much white space around the edges, and forthwith crayoned in additional decorations. He also made a little drawing for Cooper's wife. Hemingway, an old hunting companion, was on the telephone to Cooper just before he died. President Kennedy called him up. And there was a cable from the Vatican that said, "The Holy Father, fondly recalling the visit of Gary Cooper and his family, is grieved to learn of his illness and lovingly imparts a special apostolic blessing, the pledge of abundant comfort, and divine grace and favors." It was signed by Cardinal Tardini, Secretary of State of the Vatican.

Cooper's home, in the Bel-Air section of Los Angeles, was full of awards, citations, trophies and souvenirs lavished upon him during his lifetime by groups and organizations from Centralia, Illinois, to Cochin, China. Included among them were two

Academy Awards, one for his performance as *Sergeant York* and one for his role in *High Noon*. Most film stars who have won a single Academy Award put it on prominent display in their homes. Luise Rainer, who also won two, kept hers in a front window of her home in Connecticut when she lived there, where all who passed could share her triumph, or possibly resent it. Cooper, characteristically, kept his in his bedroom, out of the sight of visitors.

Cooper won those awards because of his excellence as an actor. Because many of his roles were those of a man of action who spoke only when necessary and because he so often confined his remarks to the famous and endearing foot-scuffing "Yup," many people lost sight of the fact that he was extraordinarily skilled at the trade he chose to follow. Cooper himself was inclined to make light of his own acting ability. The year before he died, he talked with the reporter Leonard Slater and said,

"Gary Cooper—an average Charlie who became a movie actor, almost reluctantly and to my very great surprise. I've made somewhere around one hundred motion pictures. Yet nothing I've done lately, the past eight years or so, has been especially worthwhile. I've been coasting along. Some of the pictures I've made recently I'm genuinely sorry about. Either I did a sloppy job in them, or the story wasn't right. I can't blame anyone for the stories that didn't come off. If I didn't get fired up about a story, why should the audience? I have to take a personal interest in my work to make it believable. And yet I can't force an interest in a character if the story has holes in it that make it illogical or unsound. When I get talked into a project I don't believe in, I'm the one who's wrong . . . not the fellow who does the talking . . ."

This was typical. His wife, Veronica, known to her friends as Rocky, has said, "A statement like that is about as much as I ever heard Gary say about his own acting. He never brought his work home from the studio, as some actors do. He was not temperamental in any way. He did not have one scrap of ham in him. To him, acting was a business. The most he might say about it was, 'I wish I'd done this a little differently . . .'"

Cooper's friends and associates felt that he always underrated himself as an actor. They pointed to such memorable films as *Mr. Deeds Goes to Town*, *Pride of the Yankees*, *Ball of Fire*, *For Whom the Bell Tolls*, *Meet John Doe*, *Sergeant York*, *A Farewell to Arms*, *The Court Martial of Billy Mitchell* and many, many others. Charles Laughton, a strict and uncompromising student of acting, declared without reservation that Cooper was among the finest actors in Hollywood. The highly-skilled Billy Wilder, acknowledged to be one of the foremost directors now living, once told a friend, "Don't be deceived by the seeming ease and naturalness of Cooper. He is a real craftsman. It is a tribute to his vast technique that he can make it all seem so easy." John Wayne, William Holden and others, even Marlon Brando, whose approach to acting was far different from Cooper's, all praised him extravagantly on occasion.

Yet it was not as an actor, primarily, that Gary Cooper captured the affection of his time. It was as a personality, as a symbol. Somehow he was able to jump out of the screen and grasp the hearts and minds of those who saw him. There was something about him that made people want to identify with him. He represented their dreams of what seemed unattainable. There was a kind of rugged nobility about this most democratic of men.

The image that he projected was that of the tall, strong, brave man of the West, or indeed of all America, for he could play soldiers and baseball players and even farmers with equal convincing validity; a man of few words, of deep thought, of capacity for tenderness and anger when he felt it necessary. It was a portrayal that made him a kind of ambassador-at-large for all America, for almost unconsciously he showed the rest of the world the very best qualities of our society. It is heartening to realize that the man himself was very like the parts he played. All his life he remained as idealistic as a high school honor student, as dedicated to principle and integrity. He was embarrassed and revolted by the tawdriness and cheapness that characterized so much of Hollywood, yet he was also quick to defend his chosen industry's good points. A lie acted upon him like a personal affront. He hated to hear stories of cheating and stealing. It would have been impossible for him to have played a villain so that people would have believed in it, for he could not have brought himself to do it sincerely. Toward the end of his life, when he was baptized in the Roman Catholic faith, he literally began to detest all the sins of his youth, as he regarded them; he felt that some of the films he had made had given young people false values and wrong notions of proper human conduct, as well as a distorted view of the men and women who had helped build the West. "He suffered greatly, for he was a genuinely religious man," a priest who was his friend has said.

He also had a quality of youthful enthusiasm that caused people to respond to him. When he was in his late fifties, and even when he was dying, he walked with a lithe, springy step, his head up, his eyes casting about inquiringly, his manner jaunty and full of quiet good humor. His mind was not restless, but he had a desire to know and understand everything that

20

caught his interest. He never could satisfy his hunger for knowledge. Joe Hyams, a Hollywood columnist who knew him well, has recalled a time in New York City when he and Cooper walked into Abercrombie and Fitch, the old sporting goods firm:

"When we got to the gun department he spent about twenty minutes hefting the weapons, looking at them with a sure and practiced eye, manipulating them with the positive touch of a man who knows what he's doing. He asked questions of the clerk about ammunition that sent the clerk scurrying to look up the answers in catalogues.

"All the while, he kept up a running conversation with the clerk that ended up with Cooper knowing more about that fellow than he ever learned about Coop . . . and the clerk was busting at the seams with questions.

"When we left—Coop ordered a gun, I forget what calibre and make—he thanked the clerk for giving him so much time. It was not a perfunctory thank-you, it was genuine."

Cooper was a crack shot. Hemingway once paid him tribute by saying he had never hunted with a better man—and the author, of course, had hunted with the best in Europe and the United States, as well as with professional white hunters in Africa. Cooper was equally good with pistol and rifle. The only time

he and Hemingway ever argued over hunting occurred one day when they fell to discussing the merits
of big-game shooting. Cooper could not bear the
thought of going after big beasts. In his view they
were too easy to hit. He preferred birds, ducks, and
small game, because he felt his quarry ought to be
permitted to match its speed and wits with his skill
and intelligence. In addition, he could not bear to kill
anything unless he planned to eat it later—he saw
nothing good in killing for its own sake. Some of his
hunting companions have said that he would only kill
enough birds for the evening meal around the camp-
fire; but if he was in an area where game was plentiful,
and he already had bagged his limit, he would go on
stalking just for the sake of being outdoors and test-
ing his ability to spot grouse, pheasant, partridge and
ducks. He was as good a shot with bow and arrow as
with firearms; he had a bow given him by the great
archer Howard Hill, one with a ninety-pound pull.

Much as Cooper loved hunting, he loved driving
an automobile more. He was considered one of the
best drivers in Hollywood, a community that is
sports-car mad. Perhaps the possession he loved most
was the huge, handsome, two-toned (dark brown
body and light brown top) Bentley he acquired the
year before he died. "I remember the day he got it,"
Hyams has said. "He was like a kid with a new toy.

He drove it to the studio one day and insisted on taking everyone out to see it. He rubbed his hands over the polished walnut dash and showed off the

He insisted on washing his cars himself.

picnic tables in the rear seat and talked about the engine with the knowledge of a salesman."

Another car Cooper loved was one he owned in the nineteen thirties, a chartreuse Deusenberg sports roadster with pea-green fenders, one of two models ever built (Clark Gable, his friend, owned the other). He gave it up after he was married. This car is now owned by the famous driver and builder of automobiles, Briggs Cunningham, and sits with the rest of his collection of classic cars in his private museum near Stamford, Connecticut. Perhaps Cooper's all-time favorite, however, was a Plymouth Fury with a Chrysler engine which he used for short hunting trips and for driving to the studio. "She'll do 120 without pausing for breath," he once told a friend. "She may not look like much, but she'll leave any other car on the road in her dust." Cooper was never a race driver, as many stars have been, but he was an expert mechanic who did much of the work on his own motors. At the same time, he insisted on washing his cars himself to make sure the job would be done exactly as he wanted it. One of his family's favorite recollections of him is his putting on an old pair of jeans and a ragged shirt and going out in the driveway of his house to wash his cars on a Saturday afternoon. He also carefully polished their chrome trimmings and vacuumed the rugs inside. He lavished similar care on every piece of sports equipment he owned. His guns were always in perfect order, cleaned and oiled and ready for firing.

During the last few years of his life, he and his wife and their daughter, Maria, became interested in skin diving. They went swimming underwater

"It's a weird feeling down there."

not only in the waters of the Pacific off Southern California, but also in the Bahamas and in the south of France. Cooper used to say with a shy grin that his wife and daughter were much more daring than he was. "They'll go down to a hundred and twenty feet," he said. "I find forty feet is deep enough for me. It's a weird feeling down there. A whole new world opens up to you." At about the same time he began skin diving he also became interested in karate. He took a few lessons from Ed Parker, a Los Angeles instructor.

Whenever Cooper became interested in any subject he made an exhaustive study of it. He knew more about the West than most university professors who have devoted their lives to researching its history. When he first became absorbed with art he filled his house with books of reproductions and began buying originals until he had amassed one of the finest privately-owned collections in the United States. Yet he did not bore his friends by talking incessantly about his hobbies. The most unostentatious of men, he kept his knowledge to himself, sharing it only with his best friends.

To the end of his life, Cooper kept a firm grip on the humility and modesty that had begun to grow in him from boyhood. A few years before he died he took a trip in a station wagon back to the Montana ranch where he spent much of his youth. He later said to his friend Hyams,

"I can tell you that when I stood at the base of the Grand Teton and looked 7,000 feet straight up and looked out over the land and thought of what the pioneers did less than 100 years ago . . . I thought, well, here I am, a big shot in the movies for a long time and maybe set on myself a bit, but I'm really not much at all. A trip like that is pretty good if you want to cut yourself down to size . . ." Nothing seemed to please this humble man more than being "cut down to size." He enjoyed telling of how, on location in a small town he had never been in before, total strangers would come up on the street thinking he was an old friend—then realize they actually did not know him, then be unable to recall his name. He liked to tell about an experience he had over and over: "There's this nice looking old lady who comes up to me and says, 'My goodness, I'd recognize you anywhere—you're the one movie actor I would know.' And then she presses her fingers to her chin and says, 'Goodness . . . what *is* your name?' That's when I know who I really am."

Cooper was too modest a man to know who he really was. He would have been astonished at the world's reaction to his passing. Pope John XXIII cabled a message to his wife and daughter, BBC broadcast a fifteen-minute tribute, and the London *Times* eulogized him in an editorial. The Cannes Film Festival went into mourning. A Tokyo newspaper critic wrote, "We feel as though we have lost our best friend." A Frankfurt newspaper said, "He was the favorite of the world." A Milan journal added, "He was a knight and a gentleman." It was his friend Clark Gable, however, who died within a few months of him, who made the simplest, truest and most definitive comment on Gary Cooper. A friend asked Gable if he knew Cooper and what he thought of him. Gable looked surprised at the question. "Why," he said, unhesitatingly, "he's a real man."

CHAPTER **2**

LAST CHANCE GULCH

Gary Cooper was descended from a long line of sturdy, adventurous, spirited men on both his mother's and his father's sides. The father, later to be known throughout Montana as Judge Cooper, came from a family of farmers who lived near the villages of the Tingrith and Houghton Regis in Bedfordshire, England. Those Coopers have been in that section for more than two centuries, and there are still two large farms being operated by people of that name. Cooper's mother, Alice Brazier, was born in Gillingham, Kent, also in England. It was a town noted for shipbuilding. The Braziers also had lived there for centuries.

General George Custer, the famous Indian fighter, who was massacred with 200-odd men by Chief Sitting Bull and his braves in Montana on June 25, 1876, was indirectly responsible for the birth of Gary Cooper.

News of this latest Indian disaster eventually reached England and was given wide coverage in the newspapers. At approximately the same time, two young men read about it—Walter Cooper in Bedfordshire and Alfred Brazier in Gillingham. Although they did not know each other and, in fact, were unaware of each other's existence, each was fired with the desire to go to America and become an Indian fighter. And each began to save his money for the passage.

The town that the young men settled in was originally called Last Chance Gulch, in the heart of the Montana Territory, which the United States had acquired as a part of the Louisiana Purchase. The development of this mineral-rich region had begun around 1852, when prospectors had found gold near Hell Gate River. Later some was discovered near Grasshopper Creek, a tributary of the Beaverhead

30

River. By the time the young Englishmen arrived, the town of Last Chance Gulch was called Helena, and it was the capital of the area—but it still was populated mainly by rough and ready miners and cowboys, most of whom carried guns. Fights broke out hourly in the muddy, unpaved streets outside the weather-battered wood frame buildings. The Indians no longer were as fierce and unruly as they once had been, but every now and then there would be a report of a tribal uprising somewhere out in the territory.

Walter Cooper lost no time in settling down to work. After a series of minor jobs he was hired on by the Northern Pacific railroad, first as a track worker, later as a worker in the shops, and eventually as a locomotive engineer. This was an enviable job in those distant days. Walter Cooper was proud of what he had achieved, and in one letter written to his relatives at home he stated that a locomotive engineer in Montana was the equal of a royal duke in Bedfordshire.

This letter was enough to send Charles Cooper, Walter's younger brother, then seventeen, into a frenzy of desire to see the New World himself. He said good-by to his parents and, with only the clothes on his back and less than an American dollar in his pocket, he went down to the sea and signed on a

merchant ship bound for New York. There he
worked at odd jobs for a time until he had saved
enough to begin heading west to Helena. It took him
nearly a year and a half to make the trip. He would
travel a bit, work a bit, and travel farther. He joined
his brother Walter in Helena in 1885. By then he
was nineteen.

There was a job for Charles on the railroad, Walter
said, but the newcomer had other plans. Men still
were settling arguments with guns, but gradually the
authorities were imposing law and order on the town.
As far as Charles could see, the rich lodes of gold,
silver, copper and other minerals would continue to
cause disputes among the prospectors. Cattlemen
were coming in to settle. They too would have disputes. There were only a few lawyers to defend the
competitors in a lawsuit, and they were fast becoming
rich.

"I've made up my mind, Walter," Charles Cooper
told his brother. "I'm going to read law."

"How can you?" Walter said. "You'll need money
—you've got none."

"I'll earn it," said Charles, and set to work. With
Walter's help he was taken on by the railroad as an
engine wiper. His hours were from six A.M. to six P.M.
It was not uncommon, in those days, for ambitious

young men to work a twelve-hour day, six days a week. Charles Cooper's energy and ambition were more than uncommon, however. He soon took on another job. At four A.M. each day he went to a local bakery, picked up a stock of bread and rolls and cakes, and went out to make deliveries. After holding down the two jobs for six months he had saved enough for his tuition at Helena's business college, where he studied law and shorthand, the latter with the intention of eventually becoming a court reporter. Even his Sundays were filled with work and study. In the morning and afternoon he would go out to solicit new customers for his baked goods, and in the late afternoon and evening he would study. An older lawyer friend advised him to read Shakespeare aloud, in order to cultivate his style of public speaking and be ready for the day when he would appear in court.

Charles sent east to a mail-order house for a one-volume edition of the works of Shakespeare. Each night, after finishing with his law studies and his shorthand exercises, he would commit a passage from one of the plays to memory. And each morning, as he made his delivery rounds, he would recite what he had memorized—to his horse. Years later he told his son, "That horse knew more Shakespeare than any other horse in Montana."

People who bought baked goods from Charles Cooper told other people about his delivery service, and he continued to look for new customers. In a few months he was earning so much from his route that he was able to quit his job in the railroad roundhouse. This provided him with an extra twelve hours each day. His first move was to make an arrangement with one of the established lawyers in the town to act as his clerk and assistant. He was a bright, quick young man with an exceptionally retentive memory, and before another year went by he had learned so much that his employer trusted him to prepare law briefs for some of his less important clients. Then too, he had mastered shorthand. Court reporters were always in demand, and he worked in the courthouse or was employed by visiting judges for several days in each month. He also had a sideline. Few of the prospectors, miners and cowboys who came into the town were able to read or write. Many of them wanted to let the folks back home know how they were doing. For a fee, Charles wrote letters for them—and for another, he read them the replies that came back.

Ironically enough, while Walter Cooper, originally a farmer, had become a railroad engineer, Alfred Brazier, who had been an engineer in England, had chosen to be a farmer. He had worked at odd jobs in the Montana town until he had saved enough to buy a little land some miles outside, and the proceeds from farming that land had helped him buy more. Soon he had a ranch of more than a hundred acres. He married and had several children. His wife helped him work the ranch; she eventually began to find that she had too much to do, and Alfred determined to write his sister in England and ask her to come out and take care of the babies.

The sister was Alice Brazier. The idea of coming to America intrigued her—but originally she planned on a short visit, just to give her brother a hand for a while. She traveled across the country by wagon and train and arrived in Helena with her return-passage money tucked safely away in her dress. Yet she never felt safe with the money concealed on her person. As soon as Alfred helped her off the train, she asked to go to a bank to deposit the money. "There are too many wild Indians and desperate men out here," she told him, "and I want to be sure I will have my fare when it's time to go home."

Alice found that she loved the wide, endless plains where her brother lived, and the massive mountains on the far horizon. She loved the way the sun turned them silver in the morning and darkened the peaks to misty purple at twilight. She learned to ride and shoot; she fed chickens and did innumerable other chores around the homestead. She was never homesick: "I never had time to be," she later said. Weeks would go by before a lone rider would pass the Brazier ranch house, but none of the family was troubled by the solitude. Nevertheless, it was Alice

They named him Frank James Cooper.

Brazier's firm intention to stay only a year. When that year was up, she thought she might lengthen her visit to another year. It was to be years before she could return to England, for one day Alfred came back from Helena with sad news.

The year was 1893. Montana had been in a state of

boom, riding a wave of prosperity thrown up by its
rich silver deposits. Men had come from all over the
country and had made fortunes. But in those days
the economy of the country was still shaky and there

were no federal regulations of markets and com-
modities such as we have today. Within a very short
time the bottom dropped out of the market. There
was a panic, and depositors made runs on the failing
banks. Every savings institution in the entire area had
to close its doors.

37

"Alice, your money is frozen," Alfred said to his sister.

"My fare? I've lost it?"

He nodded sympathetically. "I'm afraid so."

"I can't return to England?"

"Not until we can raise some money. You see, my savings are gone, too."

It was a blow for the young girl—but not as severe as it might have been. In the course of a couple of visits to Helena she had been introduced to a young man who occasionally did some legal work for her brother. His name, of course, was Charles Cooper. Through him, Alfred Brazier and Walter Cooper finally had met and become friends.

Alice thought Charles Cooper a fine man; she felt so strongly on this subject that she blushed whenever his name was mentioned. He was eight years older than she and well on his way to becoming one of the most respected men in Helena. Men were coming from a hundred miles away to give him their legal business. When her sister-in-law mentioned that Charles Cooper would make some young girl a first-rate husband, Alice blushed more deeply. As for Charles Cooper, he was thinking that it was about time to get married. He wanted to settle down with a family; he wanted sons to carry on the name and to help in the future development of this new land.

In the spring of 1962, Mrs. Alice Brazier Cooper was eighty-eight years old. She still recalled her courting days as vividly as though they had occurred in the spring of 1961. She remembered that young Lawyer Cooper had come riding out to the Brazier ranch for several Sundays in a row, and that on one visit he had asked her if she might like to go fishing with him. When they came back from that afternoon's trip they were engaged.

Mrs. Cooper told a friend, "Everybody said, 'Alice went fishing with Charlie—and she didn't catch any fish, but she caught Charlie.' "

The couple's first son, Arthur, was born in 1895.

Six years later, on May 7, 1901, Alice gave birth to a second son. She and her husband named him Frank James Cooper.

CHAPTER 3

DUNSTABLE

The old stagecoach driver was sitting on the bench by the railroad station, his favorite spot, squinting in the sun and whittling. Little Frank Cooper, who was about six years old and sun-bronzed as an Indian, was sitting beside him. Nearly every day after school the boy would go over and sit with the old man, listening to his stories. It did not matter to him that he had heard them more times than he could remember. "Tell me about the Plummer boys," he would say.

Spitting a stream of tobacco juice, the old man

would shake his head. "I must have told you that story about a thousand times, boy."

"Tell it again—please. Tell about the time they held you up."

The old man liked to tell the story, but he pretended that it bored him. He whittled away for a moment. Then he began.

"When I was drivin' the stage, I had the run from Helena to Virginia City. Now, let me tell you, Virginia City, Montana, was the toughest town in the whole wide West. They talk about Dodge City, Kansas. Humph. It warn't nothin' compared to Virginia City. Why, boy, a man from Dodge wouldn'ta *dared* go into that town. Even the wolves roamin' the plains around there wouldn't go too close—the Virginia City dogs was too tough. Them dogs would of plumb run the wolves out.

"And the way them fellers up there fought each other—the richest man in town was the undertaker. They made their own bullets, those Virginia men— and when the castin' didn't come out good and proper for their guns, they'd file 'em smooth by rubbin' 'em agin their teeth.

"Why, you couldn't even say 'Howdy' to one o' them Virginia City boys without takin' your life in your hands, that's how tough they was. And mean. And ornery."

The boy's striking blue eyes grew large. "Now tell about the Plummer boys."

"Them Plummer boys," said the old man, "was the worst of all the men in Virginia City. Ain't no way o' tellin' how many banks they robbed in the Montana territory, how many men they killed, how many stages they held up. They was especially good at holdin' up stages." He paused significantly. "Except my stage."

"Tell about the time you held them off," the boy begged.

"Well, boy, it was twelve, thirteen year ago. I was drivin' the noon stage from Virginia City to here. Had two or three women aboard and a couple o' men. Swells. Fine, fancy clothes, luggage look like it come all the way from St. Louis. Also, I had the mail, and I had a box on that stage that had had high as *five thousand dollars'* o' silver inta it.

"Them Plummer boys had run up a string o' hold-ups just about the time I'm tellin' about, and a lot of stage drivers didn't want to take a chance o' gettin' caught by 'em. So they quit—just plumb quit. Not me. I made up my mind no Plummer boys was goin' to a-scare *me*.

"Well, I started out at noon, right on schedule. Drove about two hours, nothin' happened. Then I came to this pass goin' through a couple o' rocky hills,

42

"I pulled my gun before them bandits knew it."

and next thing I knew I heard a *Crack* and a bullet buzzed right by my head. The Plummers, sure as shootin'. And there they were, two of 'em, wearin' masks black as midnight, standin' on their horses right in the middle of the road. Then I looked around up on the rocks and there were more of 'em, all with their guns pointed right at me. That's a thing that's bad on a man's nerves. There must of been a dozen.

" 'Put up your hands!' one of them Plummers yelled at me. Well, that was the silliest durn thing I ever heard in my life. If I'd of put up my hands, I'd

43

of lost control of my team, wouldn't I? So I just give a laugh and took the reins in my left hand and slapped my horses backs smart-like, and with my right hand I found my gun and pulled it afore them bandits knew what was happenin'. I just drove that stage lickety-split right toward those two desperadoes there in the center o' the road, and meanwhile I took some shots at the ones up on the rocks. The two on horseback scattered—their horses reared back and threw 'em. And I'm pretty sure I picked off four o' the rest with my Colt. And that was how I got the stage through the Plummer boys. Couple days later, the marshal went out there and rounded 'em up. They never give nobody any trouble after that . . ."

Stories of that kind, told first-hand by the men who experienced them, were important parts of Frank Cooper's boyhood. And so were the scenes that went on around him every day in that frontier town. By the time he was six, his father had taken a good-sized, substantial house, suitable for a lawyer's family, a two-story brick house that faced on Eleventh Avenue and backed up against Last Chance Gulch. His mother was determined to preserve "civilized" ways, and his father was determined to be "respectable." But young Frank had other ideas and enjoyed other pursuits.

The Indians were his friends, and most of the time

he behaved like an Indian, his mother has recalled. His older brother, Arthur, who today is a bank president, was sober and serious-minded, but Frank ran wild all over Helena and the countryside around. His mother forbade him to go into the main streets of the town on Saturday afternoons, when the men came in from their ranches and mines to get provisions. There was drinking then, and fights always broke out. Mrs. Cooper felt that it was dangerous for Frank to go there—but sometimes his curiosity would get the better of him and he would sneak away and wander down into the town. One of Cooper's most vivid impressions in later years was a fight in a livery stable he saw one Saturday afternoon: two big men, both intoxicated, fought for nearly two hours, knocking each other down time and again. Finally, their faces battered, blood streaming all over their clothes, they stopped and shook hands—and went down the street to a saloon to buy each other drinks.

On Saturdays and Sundays, the boy sometimes went on long rides into the countryside, loping along on a pony rented from the livery stable. In the summers, at the ranch that his father had bought, a huge spread about sixty miles outside the town, he rode his own grey-and-white pony over the plains and into the mountains. He liked to play at being a prospector and made himself a small pan with which

45

he would wash the sand in the streams up in the mountains. The prospectors had long since taken most of the gold out of those streams, but sometimes in the spring, after the floods had washed over the sand again, Frank and his friends found tiny grains of gold which they would take to the general store in Helena and trade for caramels, licorice, jaw breaker balls and other candy. Sometimes, too, he would wander around looking for Indian arrowheads, for there had been many battles in that section only about twenty years previously. Other days he would take his sling shot, which a prospector had taught him to make, and go hunting jackrabbit, partridge, and other animals and birds. He became a first-rate huntsman with the sling shot, and later on an Indian couple who took care of his father's ranch in the winter taught him to make bows and arrows. When he was twelve, his father gave him his first rifle; he picked it up and began firing it as though he had been shooting it all his life.

At the ranch, Frank kept rabbits, chickens, and, wild birds he caught in his wanderings. His friends were the four sons of the Indian couple who worked for the family. They used to hunt or fish together. He fished for trout in the clear mountain streams, sleeping overnight in the forest in a rolled-up blanket, getting up at dawn to cast into the rushing, sparkling

He and the Indian boys would fish for trout.

waters. Later he and the Indian boys would build a fire and fry the trout, roasting potatoes in the coals.

Their life was not all hunting and fishing and riding. Lawyer Cooper was determined to build a sense of responsibility into his sons, and thus Frank was given a full complement of chores to do every day. In the morning he was expected to feed the chickens, ducks, and geese and his rabbits, and to clean the latters' hutches. He fed the cows and horses, too, and swept out the stables. Watching his father, and imitating him, he became a capable carpenter and wagon mechanic.

Nor did Lawyer Cooper neglect his sons' classical education. Each evening after dinner he would take down his worn volume of Shakespeare and read to the boys passages that he especially admired and wanted them to know by heart. He also read frequently to them from the Bible and recited long passages of poetry that he had committed to memory as a diversion while he was engaged in the prosaic business of learning the law. As far as his mother could recall in later years, this exposure to Shakespeare did nothing whatever to instill in her son the desire to be an actor. Nor did their regular attendance at the Episcopal Church seem to stimulate him into any special preoccupation with religion. Mrs. Cooper once told a friend she believed that her boy actually would have preferred running with his Indian friends on Sunday mornings.

It was Frank's fondness for his Indian companions that began to worry her when he was about nine. It was not that she was prejudiced against the Indians; on the contrary, she liked them. But she had come from a most proper English family, and she was determined to raise her boys properly. She always had been a forward-looking woman, and she was concerned for their future. What alarmed her most was Frank's table manners. Like many boys, he was impatient at the table. He had an enormous appetite, but he regarded a meal as something to be disposed of as quickly as possible. Also, he sometimes would come to the table with dirty hands; he always seemed to "forget" that his mother insisted upon cleanliness. It was a losing battle; she always sent him out to wash up. At the table, too, there were constant cries of, "Frank! Merciful Heavens, will you mind your manners?" She tried to teach him the English style of holding his knife and fork, but he never could seem to master it—which was odd, for in other ways he was extremely dexterous.

Then, one day about two years later, came the last straw. By hanging around the old stagecoach driver

49

and other old-timers who loafed around Helena, Frank had picked up a somewhat picturesque vocabulary. Swearing was strictly forbidden in his home, but outside he often tried to talk like the adults he admired. One day, as he was doing a small repair job on a chair in the kitchen, he hit his finger with a hammer and uttered one of the words he had heard his older friends using. Mrs. Cooper grabbed him by the ear, led him to the sink, and washed his mouth out with strong soap and water.

That evening, after dinner, Alice Cooper had a conversation with her husband. Her boys were becoming savages, she said. It was a sin and a shame, what was happening to them. Why, they would grow up without a scrap of culture in their lives! Whatever would become of them?

Lawyer Cooper nodded as she counted off each point. Also, he agreed that perhaps the education available at the little one-room school in Helena possibly could have been improved upon.

So it was decided. Arthur and Frank were to be taken to England and put into school. They protested vainly. For a time, Frank even thought of running away from home and trying to get a job on a ranch where his parents would not be able to find him. After all, he reasoned, there was probably some ranch somewhere that would have a berth for a good

They were not prepared for whispers of "Sissy!"

almost-twelve-year-old cowpoke. But somehow he never could seem to muster up the equipment he would need to run away.

Mother and sons sailed for England. From the first sight of the grey buildings in the English cities, the boys were horribly depressed. "Where are the plains?" Frank asked. "Where are the mountains?" asked Arthur.

"You will learn to love this country," their mother said.

She was wrong. They were so homesick that they could scarcely talk. Their appetites went off; they found the food strange-tasting and flat. There were none of the thick steaks they were used to in Helena, and the roast beef tasted peculiar. They lost weight and they lost spirit. After three months their mother took them back to Montana.

Mrs. Alice Cooper was a determined lady. The boys instantly lapsed back into their old habits. They ran wild, they forgot their manners, they were only mildly interested in school, although Arthur was more interested than his younger brother.

"We are going to try again," Mrs. Cooper told her husband. Again, he was agreeable. And again they went to the United Kingdom.

Now began what Cooper later looked back on as the worst period of his life. His mother enrolled him at Dunstable, a public school noted for its high academic standards. They were so high, in fact, they were completely out of Frank Cooper's sight. The headmaster intimidated him on his first day.

"How much Latin have you had?"

"Why . . . I don't know."

"You don't know how much Latin you've had, young sir?"

"I just plain don't even know what Latin *is*."

Cooper was equally at a loss when it came to French, algebra and other subjects. The school in Helena had taught little more than reading, writing, and arithmetic, and he had not paid very strict attention to those subjects, principally because his mind had been on what he considered more important topics, such as hunting and fishing.

"We will get tutors for you," the headmaster said.

The lad was terribly embarrassed. He was put in a form with boys three years younger than he was, all of whom knew much, much more than he did. He felt ashamed of his awkward American pronunciation of the language; some of his fellow students, and even some of his teachers, could not understand the way he talked. Then too, while the friends he did manage to make were out after school playing soccer, tag, cricket or rugby football, he was forced to sit with a tutor and try to catch up in his studies. Most

53

of all, he hated the uniform—the short jacket, the tight long pants, and the crowning indignity, the traditional top hat.

Much as he hated the school and the life he was forced to lead in England, far removed from his beloved ranch, Cooper managed to stick to his studies for three years. And, somewhat to his surprise, he also managed to do fairly well in them. He won a school prize toward the end of his second year for having shown the most improvement, and wrote a letter home to his father couched in careful composition-class phrases. But toward the middle of his third year, to his great joy his mother decided that three years of the English school would be enough. Also, she missed her husband and wanted to get back to the ranch just as much as her sons did. They sailed for America and reached Helena just the day before the fall term of the school there was to start.

Boys can grow a good deal in three years, and all the Coopers had to wear were their Dunstable uniforms. Therefore, when the school bell rang that morning, they turned up wearing their top hats. They had become so used to the English garb they had forgotten how odd it would look to their old friends, and they were not prepared for the jeers and the whispers of, "Sissy! Snobs!" Young Frank, whose disposition was considerably more volatile than that

54

of his older brother, was especially angered. Right after school was out, he gave chase after the boys who had teased him and caught up with a group. One by one he took them on, receiving in succession a black eye, a broken front tooth, a bloody nose, another black eye, and assorted bruises around the cheeks, chest and upper arms. When he finally got home, some three hours later, his mother all but fainted. He had been beaten badly but he was happy and grinning. Every last piece of his English clothing had been torn off, and he never would be able to wear them again. That night he went to bed happier than he had been for three years.

CHAPTER 4

CHARCOAL AND PAD

All during his three years in school in England, young Frank Cooper had impressed his teachers with the drawings he made—and had exasperated some of them, too, for he persisted in doing the drawings on pads when he should have been studying his Latin and algebra. At the age of nine, he had decided that he would be an artist when he grew up.

Just before Mrs. Cooper took her sons to England, Lawyer Cooper had become Judge Cooper. His neighbors' respect for him was so great they had

named him to the Montana State Supreme bench—
and one morning Frank was taken by his mother to
see his father in the state capitol in his chambers.
Minerals had made Montana rich, and the capitol
building was a truly imposing structure. The building
itself, however, was not what awed the little boy—it
was a mural that spread all across the huge lobby, a
painting called *Lewis and Clark at Ross Hole*, by the
great painter of Western scenes, Charles Russell.
Nearly forty years later, in his autobiography, written
in collaboration with George Scullin, Cooper told of
the tremendous impact the painting had on him at
that age.

"I was stopped, really nailed in my tracks," he
said. ". . . It showed explorers, Indians and horses,
and every one of them seemed ready to pick right up
and move past me . . . Years later I discovered that
the mural is one of Russell's masterpieces, but all I
knew then, as a youngster, was that I would give
anything to be able to paint like that . . ."

Mrs. Cooper has recalled that he came home ex-
citedly from the visit to the capitol and promptly sat
down and began to draw. Later, when he returned
from England, he never went out on a pack trip on
his pony without taking along a sketch pad and a few
bits of charcoal that he had made for himself by burn-
ing wood. He would sit in thickets by the hour,

He would sit by the hour with his charcoal and pad.

silently stalking wild birds with his charcoal and pad, and later he would take his drawings home and respectfully ask the Judge what he thought of them. Although after he became an actor he gave up this hobby, he remained interested in fine art until the end of his life. His daughter, Maria, who was encouraged by her father at an early age, is today a good artist in her own right.

As Cooper recalled it many years afterward, he felt some frustration in his artistic ambitions when he was a boy, for he never had enough time to practice. While he and his brother and mother were in England, his father had begun to develop the ranch, which was called Seven Bar Nine. It was a spread of bottom land, shaped like a crescent moon, bounded on the east by the Missouri River and on the west by the Rockies. It was a mile long and a half-mile wide, and along with it were thousands and thousands of acres of stock-grazing area that Judge Cooper had leased from the government. When the three Coopers came home from England, they saw to their amazement that the head of their family had put in a good-sized herd of cattle and had built not only a ranch house but several barns, outbuildings and corrals.

"You boys," said Judge Cooper, "are going to own all this when you're grown—so you'd better learn about it now."

Arthur Cooper never had a chance to learn. World War I broke out, and all at once all the cowboys, Indians, sharecroppers and other ranch hands who were working on Seven Bar Nine were caught up by the desire to go and, in the popular phrase of the day, make the world safe for democracy. Arthur Cooper felt the same way. He enlisted.

"Dad, can't I enlist too?" Frank asked the Judge.

"I approve of your spirit, son," said the Judge, "but you're a little young, I'm afraid—and someone has got to stay and help your mother take care of the ranch." The Judge was too busy with his state work on the bench to devote any time to the ranch, and because all the outside help had gone off to war, the job was left to the mother and the remaining son.

During the next two years, two significant events occurred in the life of Frank James Cooper.

The first was that he made up his mind, beyond any doubt whatever, that much as he loved the out-doors, much as he loved the ranch itself, he would never become a ranch owner. He and his mother chopped up frozen bales of hay with axes at twenty degrees below zero at five A.M., and then he would hitch up a team and take the hay out through six-foot drifts of snow to the herd of cattle on the range. They had to thaw ice to get drinking water. They were thankful when spring was in sight—but they reckoned without the chinook, a warm wind that came down from the mountains and melted all the snow and ice into a flood that broke a nearby dam and inundated their property.

The ranch house stood firm, but all other buildings were swept away. Moreover, the flood deposited a foot-deep layer of sand, gravel and stones over the hayfield on which Cooper and his mother had planned to grow feed for their cattle.

The following year the rains arrived: twenty-eight days and twenty-eight nights' worth, and this time the floods finished the job on the Cooper ranch.

"So much for the ranch business," Judge Cooper said, laconically, and subsequently turned it over to a family of tenant farmers.

The second significant event was caused by the hard work that led to his deciding that he was not cut out to be a ranch owner. In thirteen months he grew thirteen inches. Before Arthur went away to war, he had towered over Frank. Now that he was back, he was a good head shorter.

In order to keep the ranch running, Frank had quit school temporarily. With the armistice signed, the Indians and ranch hands came back to work again, and he began to think about resuming his education. There was one handicap: his size. The boys in school in his class were all only about half as tall as he was, and he now felt awkward to be sitting there with them. One day he summoned his courage, overcame his shyness, and told his troubles to a sympathetic teacher, a Miss Wheeler, who had perceived that he did not seem interested in his studies and had wondered what was wrong.

"These others are so small, I feel out of place here," he said.

"What do you think you want to do with your life, Frank?"

"Well, ma'am, I had thought some about becoming an artist. I can sketch a little in charcoal, and my water colors aren't too dreadful."

"No, they're very good indeed," she said. "Perhaps there is an answer for you. At Wesleyan here in Helena, they have courses you could take that might enable you to go to Montana State, at Bozeman, in the fall. Why don't you enroll and see what happens?"

Frank was quick to take her advice. After spending two semesters at Wesleyan he matriculated at Montana State. In the summers he worked on ranches as a cowpoke, saving money to continue his education. His dream was to go east to school; he had seen England and had not liked it, but he was eager to see what the rest of his country looked like.

Before he entered Montana State, he was in an

Both boys went straight up into the air.

accident the aftereffects of which changed his life and made it possible for him to become a movie actor . . . although, of course, he had no notion then of what it ultimately would mean.

His best friend at Wesleyan was another Helena boy, Harvey Markham. Some years before, Harvey had had polio. He was paralyzed from the waist down, but his father had equipped a Model T Ford with hand controls, and Harvey could drive as well as anyone. Each morning he would pick up Cooper and drive him to school.

One morning they were riding along as usual when they came to the crest of a steep hill on the outskirts of Helena. About a third of the way down, Harvey grabbed the lever that operated the foot brake. It did not respond. The car began to gather speed. "Hang on!" Harvey cried, and grabbed the lever for the hand brake. It came away. At the bottom of the hill there was a sharp turn to the left, and beyond that a gully. They were heading straight for it, and it seemed certain they would crash; in desperation, Harvey yanked at the lever for reverse gear. Like the foot brake, it came off in his hand. Terror in his face, he tried to wrestle the plunging Ford around the corner, but his turn was too sharp. The wheels turned so abruptly, the rear end of the car flew up and both boys went straight up in the air, splitting the flimsy canvas top with their heads and hurtling high above the roadbed. Harvey was thrown clear and escaped with only a few bumps and brushburns. Cooper, for a split-second, thought he was in the clear, too, but as he watched, the car, standing on its radiator, fell on top of him. "It seemed to take a long, long time to make up its mind to fall," he later said.

There was not much medical equipment in Helena. The doctors poked and prodded the youngster and decided that rest would get him back in shape before very long. "Just a few torn ligaments in the hip," they said. "No bones broken—nothing serious."

Frank was out of the hospital within a week. He had begged the doctors to let him go up to the Seven Bar Nine to rest, and they had agreed. He was not there a day before he was defying their instructions and walking on crutches—and a few days later he pulled himself up on a docile horse and went out for a ride.

The trouble was, riding the horse hurt his hip almost as much as walking on crutches had. Soon he learned to favor the hip as he rode, shifting his weight as the horse moved so that the hip would not be jarred. Previously he had been a good, but careless, rider; now, keeping the hip from hurting, he became as one with the horse. And in that way he developed the riding skill that was to make him far and away the finest **rider** among all the cowboy stars. Yet, by all that is reasonable, this never should have happened. Nearly fifteen years after the accident, when he was well-established as an actor, a scene in a picture called for him to fall off a horse. Cooper never permitted stunt men to work in his place unless the studio executives absolutely insisted upon it. This seemed like a routine fall—but when he got up, the same hip that had been hurt in the accident with Harvey Markham began to ache unbearably. The studio doctor sent him to a hospital, and a bone specialist came in to make an examination. Naturally, X-rays were taken. A bit later the specialist arrived with the plates in his hand.

"Where did you get *this?*" he asked. He held up the plate. There was a huge crack in Cooper's hip.

"Oh, I guess that must be that Harvey Markham accident," Cooper said, shrugging. "It happened when I was in college back home . . . wasn't much." He told the story. When he told about going riding while he was recuperating, the doctor could not believe him.

"You actually went *horseback* riding?"

"All the time."

"It's a wonder you weren't a cripple for life."

"It just shows you what ignorance will do for a kid," Cooper said, grinning.

The accident did more than teach him to ride. His

period of recuperation gave him the solitude he needed—to practice his drawing, to read, and to think. It seemed to him during that period, in which he was completely alone, that he had to come to some decision about his life. "Except for the way this hip hurts—and that ought to be over soon—I'm about as happy here as I've ever been," he thought. Nothing he ever had experienced had given him more pleasure than sitting quietly and sketching the wondrously beautiful country all around him and the creatures that lived on it. He made up his mind. No matter how long it would take him, he would go to school and study, and one day he would be an artist.

CHAPTER 5

YELLOWSTONE GUIDE

During interviews he gave after he was a star, Gary Cooper loved to tell how Frank Cooper had failed to be admitted to the drama club when he was in college. But after his death his mother remembered an incident that he evidently had forgotten.

"Daddy encouraged him to develop a taste for public speaking," she recalled. "He tried out in a few declamation contests, and he was good enough to enter into the state competitions. He always came out near the top. But then, one year, the Helena school was putting on a play. It was called, as I remember, *The Upright Piano*. The English teacher was the director. She was anxious for him to play one of the major roles, but he refused. The truth is, he was too shy!"

In 1921, having amassed enough credits at Wesleyan and Montana State to continue his college career elsewhere, Frank James Cooper set out by train for Grinnell College, in Grinnell, Iowa. To him, this section of the country, which most people thought of as the Midwest, was so far from Montana that he considered it the East.

Almost as soon as he arrived in Grinnell he became conscious, all over again, that he was an outsider and something of a misfit. He was three years older than most of the young people in his class, and much taller —and they all had gone through school in a normal manner. In classes his shyness helped make him feel as though he was mentally, as well as chronologically, retarded. He kept to himself, spending most of his time in his room studying hard to catch up. For a time he considered going out for the football team, but the hip injury, which still bothered him, put an end to that notion.

Soon after the semester began, he heard that one

of the professors was looking for an all-around handy man to do some chores after classes each day. He sought out the man, applied for the job, and was hired at once. The professor had an apple orchard, and it was Cooper's task at first to pick up the apples that had fallen from the trees and run them through a cider press, then bottle the cider and store it away in his employer's cellar.

One day Cooper's roommate, a lad who was majoring in chemistry, came home with a book on distilling he had found in the library. When Cooper came in, he showed him the book and suggested they take some of the professor's apple cider and try to distill it.

"Oh, I don't know if we ought to do that," Cooper said, dubiously.

The student was a very persuasive talker. He said that the experiment would help him in his chemistry classes, and finally Cooper agreed. That afternoon he brought home a gallon of apple juice, and the roommate forthwith put it into a crude still he had made with equipment from the laboratory.

After a time, all the juice had been run through the still, and what came out was a clear white fluid that looked no more harmful than water.

"Here," said the student, "since you got the juice, you're entitled to the first drink."

Cooper had never had a drink of alcoholic beverage of any kind in his life. His father had never taken more than a glass of wine just preceding Christmas dinner. He was far from prepared for the applejack. Nevertheless, he picked up the glass and took a good-sized gulp.

The sensations, he later said, were impossible to describe. First it was as though someone had put a hot poker in his mouth and held it on his tongue. Then it was as though the poker had set fire to his throat, to his gullet, and finally, to his stomach. And down in that organ there was an explosion that zoomed up and made him feel as though his head was flying off. Tears came into his eyes, he began to cough, and then dizziness overcame him. He thought he would faint.

"Gee," said the roommate, "that sure must be strong."

Cooper sat down weakly on his bed. He could not speak; all he could manage was a feeble nod. It was the last drink he had for many years, and from that point on he had to force himself to go work every day for the professor. Even the smell of apple juice made him queasy.

Judge Charles Cooper had advanced his son the cost of his tuition for his first year. By working for the professor and taking other odd jobs, Frank Cooper

71

was able to save enough to pay back the loan and to get a good start toward his tuition for the following year. He considered returning to Helena for the summer and working the ranch, but then a letter came from his father telling him he had leased it out to another rancher. An important legal case had come up, one that eventually would bring him enough money to retire. Therefore, he and his wife were moving to Los Angeles for a time. He was retiring from his judgeship.

Almost at the same time, Cooper had a letter from his friend Harvey Markham. Some of the boys were signing on as guides and handy men in the national parks. This sounded like a good idea, and he wrote the authorities at Yellowstone National Park applying for a job. After a time a letter came back saying that all guide positions were filled, but there was an opening for a bus driver. Although he had never driven a bus, he decided to give it a try.

He arrived at Yellowstone in mid-June, was welcomed by the foreman, and installed in a bunkhouse with the rest of the hands. It looked like a good setup, and he was facing the prospect of a pleasant, and profitable, summer. Then his boss took him out to see the bus. He could scarcely believe his eyes. It was a ten-passenger open-air vehicle that looked as though it was held together with bits of string and rubber bands. Even when it was standing still, he later recalled, it seemed to rattle. The seats were bolted loosely to the floor. The driver's seat had long since vanished and had been replaced by an old camp chair. The roads around Yellowstone were rocky, and the original springs had been replaced by a set that apparently had been pried off a prairie schooner. In addition, there was a ratchet shift. In order to get from one gear to the other, the driver had to get the bus up to the proper speed and, at the strategic moment, ram the shift into the proper position—but if he missed, the gearbox was likely to fall apart. "It might give you a little trouble until you get used to it," said the foreman, "especially on the hills." Cooper looked around. It seemed to him there were no flat stretches; as far as he could see, there were hills.

The bus shuddered as he climbed into the camp stool. He looked around for the self-starter.

"You got to crank it," said the foreman.

On the first try, Cooper was pitched four feet backward. He landed in a sitting position, wondering what happened.

"It's ornery, all right," the foreman said.

Presently he got it started and ran around to climb into the stool. As soon as he sat down, the motor died.

This went on for about fifteen minutes. Passengers for a sight-seeing trip had begun to collect. Their smiles and whispers did not improve his disposition. After he had cranked it and it had died for what seemed like the twentieth time, he lost his patience and temper. As he was going up front, he gave the front wheel a vicious kick. This time the bus started quite peaceably. The passengers climbed into the unsteady seats, and they started out.

Cooper soon found that when the foreman had said "hills," he actually had meant "mountains." The road went up, up, and up, wound around hair-raising precipices, and went up, up, and up again. There was one elevation called Canyon Wall, 10,000 feet in the air, from which the road led down—almost straight down, he later recalled—to another straightaway, 5,000 feet below. The course was plainly marked, and so was his face—with fear. He held on to the wheel as though his hands had been nailed to it. The passengers held to each other in terror; most of them closed their eyes, forgetting that they had come out sight-seeing.

Somehow he got the bus back to the main base. The foreman was standing there, shaking his head.

"You notice?" he said. "No tips."

"Tips? What do you mean?"

"Gosh, man, you don't expect to get by this sum-

"You'll never be an actor."

mer just on your wages, do you? These people are tourists. They got money to spend. Most drivers get as high as two dollars in tips per ride."

"But how?"

"You got to act scared."

"Act scared? I was scared, almost out of my wits."

"Now, I don't mean that," the wily supervisor said. "What I mean is, you got to make 'em glad they got back here alive—and they'll be so grateful to you for bringin' 'em, they'll give you a tip. When you go around one o' them corners up there, yell somethin' like, 'Hang on!' or 'Don't know if we'll make this one—get ready to jump!' "

Cooper gulped. "That's what I felt like yelling anyhow!"

"All right, then, just act natural," the foreman said.

On the next trip out, Cooper punctuated every turn and every bouncy descent of the rocky road with loud shouts. The passengers responded with shouts of their own. "Let me off!" one man yelled. "I'll walk back!" At the end of the ride, the grateful tourists passed a hat. Net for Frank Cooper: $1.75. And so he spent the summer, driving and shouting.

Grinnell looked better to him that fall. He had saved enough to pay not only his tuition but his room and board, and he had more time to himself. The only difficulty was that he still did not feel at ease with his fellow students.

"You ought to get yourself some kind of outside interest," his chemistry-major roommate said. "Why don't you try out for one of the clubs?"

"I'm already a member of the art club," Cooper said.

"That's what I mean—you already know all the people in that club. Why don't you try for one where you don't know anybody? Why don't you try out for the dramatics club?"

Cooper looked at his friend as though he had gone crazy. "What would I do with that bunch? I can't act."

"Neither can they."

Tryouts for aspiring members were to be held the following night. Cooper turned up, reluctantly and nervously, for he still wondered what he was doing there. The group was directed by a woman who had had some stage experience before settling down to the life of a teacher. She listened to each student impatiently, accepting and rejecting them with jerks of her thumb. Presently it was the turn of the gangling lad from Montana. She handed him a book. "Read those lines," she commanded.

Cooper took the book in his big hands. Nervousness overcame him; the pages were shaking before his eyes. He felt a dryness in his mouth. He tried to speak and could not produce a sound.

The lady snatched the book away. "That's enough," she said. "What ever prompted you to come to this club?"

"Well," he began, miserably, "my friend said . . ."

"Never mind. You'd better try some other club. As long as you live, Mr. Cooper, you'll never be an actor."

CHAPTER **6**

CORRAL BUZZARD

During the second half of his second year at Grinnell, Cooper gradually came to the conclusion that he was wasting his time. He was doing well enough in his art studies. From water colors he had graduated to oils, and had done some fair ranch scenes that had brought him the approval of his teachers. But in his other studies he was floundering. He was still obsessed by the notion that he was far, far behind his fellow students. He did not seem to be able to concentrate on anything but art. One day, he saw a Chicago art school's listing in a magazine and sent off for a catalogue. This place seemed ideal for him. It offered courses in color, design, technique, sculpture—everything he felt he needed if he was to be another Charles Russell. The school had only one disadvantage, as far as he could see. The tuition was about twice that of Grinnell.

At Yellowstone Park the summer before he had earned just about as much as there was to be made. It would take him two summers there to accumulate enough money to transfer to Chicago. He considered asking his father for a loan, but decided against it; the Judge would give him the money, he knew, but he wanted to try to earn it on his own. However, he knew he could live at home without paying board, and if he could get a job in the Los Angeles area, perhaps he could save enough during the summer to enter the art school in the autumn. Back he went, at the end of the term, to Los Angeles.

While at Grinnell, encouraged by one of his instructors, he had sent some cartoons off to the Helena *Independent*, and to his great joy the editor had published a few of them. Inspired by these easy accomplishments, he was certain that the editors of Los Angeles newspapers would welcome him. He was wrong. There were no situations for young cartoonists on any of the Los Angeles newspapers. At least, there was no situation for him. The drawings were not bad, but they were not good enough.

"I think you need experience, young man," one editor said. "Tell you what—go down to the advertising department. They might have something for you down there."

Drawings under his arm, Cooper went to see the head of the display advertising section. He was taken on at once, but on a conditional basis.

"Here is a list of advertisers we are trying to get into the paper," the man said. "Draw some possible advertisements for these people, take them around, and if you sell them the space you get a commission."

Cooper ran all the way home. When he got there he waved the list in his mother's face. "I've got a job! I'm on a newspaper!"

A moment later, when he took a close look at the list, he was not so certain that he would have a job. The firms he was to solicit were hair-removing parlors, one-room outfits offering cures for baldness, wigmakers, smoking cure establishments, and tattoo emporiums. Most of those businesses had trouble paying their rents. Nevertheless, he bravely set to work sketching advertisements and went around trying to sell them. For days he walked the street, going from one fly-by-night operation to the next. He met some odd and interesting people. One tattooist offered to put an American flag on his chest in return for some advertising space, but that was as near to success as he came.

"I think," said his mother, "you'd better look for something else, Frank."

For three weeks, working as an outside representative for a photographer, he walked the streets and rang doorbells, offering to make arrangements to have housewives' children photographed in their homes. He was to get fifty per cent of the sales he made. He made none.

The next job was as assistant to a man who painted commercial backdrop curtains for vaudeville theatres. These curtains were familiar in theatres all over the country during the second and third decades of this century. The painter would go to merchants in the neighborhood of the theatre and sell them space on a curtain, and then he would decorate the curtain with panels telling about barber shops, grocery stores, cleaners and dyers and the like. Cooper found out, after working for a couple of weeks, that there was less demand for this form of advertising than there was for newspaper space.

At the beginning of the summer he had had a little money left over from a few part-time jobs at Grinnell. Now the summer was almost gone, and so were his savings. The fall came on. He could not find a job, not even as a grocery clerk; every time a potential employer learned that he intended to go to school as soon as he had enough money saved, his chances for employment vanished.

"Something will turn up, son," his mother kept saying.

Nothing did. He kept walking the streets and hounding the employment agencies. If he had not told interviewers that he hoped to go to school, he could have had any one of a number of jobs—but he was far too honest for that. It never occurred to him to conceal his plans.

One day he was ambling along Hollywood Boulevard, heading for an employment agency he had not yet tried, when he passed two fellows whose faces looked familiar. They stopped in amazement. "Well, I'll be!" one shouted. "Frank Cooper!" Simultaneously, Cooper emitted a shout of surprise. Jimmy Calloway and Jimmy Galen were boys he had known in Montana.

They were in cowboy clothes—and, Cooper later remembered, they looked terrible. He could not understand it. They were both lawyers' sons, as he was, but their fathers were far more prosperous than his ever had been.

"You guys look as though you've been in a fight," Cooper said, as the three of them automatically headed into a diner for a cup of coffee.

"Fight, heck," said Calloway. "These are our workin' clothes."

"What kind of jobs have you got that make you look like that?"

"It's a long story," Galen said, as he ordered coffee. "You remember Slim Talbot, don't you?"

"Do I!" Cooper exclaimed. "What's happened to him?"

Jay Talbot, called Slim by all his friends, had been one of Cooper's boyhood idols in Helena. By the time he was fifteen he was a legend in his own neighborhood, for he already had begun to win rodeo contests by the score. Around Helena he was known as the best horseman in all Montana, the best roper, and the best bulldogger. He was about five years older than Cooper, and by the time he was eighteen he had won nearly every rodeo prize offered in the Western states. When World War I came he had become a flyer, and afterward he had taken to performing at rodeos and fairs, doing exhibitions in the air with his own plane and winning prizes with his horse on the ground. Eventually he made his way to Hollywood.

"Calloway and I were travelin' with a rodeo," Jimmy Galen explained. "Business wasn't so good.

84

We were stranded, and we had nothin' to do but go back to Helena. Well, sir, somebody back home told us old Slim Talbot was out here, workin' in the movin' pictures. We wrote to him to ask if he thought there might be any jobs for a couple of cowhands who weren't too bad at ridin', and he wrote back sayin' come ahead. So here we are."

Cooper stared at his old friends for a long time before he spoke. "You don't mean to tell me you're . . . *actors?*"

"Well, not exactly," Calloway said. "They call us 'cowboy extras.' It's just like the rodeo only in reverse. Instead of stickin' onto a horse, we fall off. We don't bulldog steers . . . they more or less bulldog us. And we do it in front of cameras. Sometimes we chase each other. Some days we're good guys, some days we're bad guys. If we break any bones, the studio pays for it."

"Ten dollars a day," Galen added, proudly.

Cooper's heart gave a jump. Ten dollars a day! Why, with a couple of months' work, he could raise all the money he needed for Chicago.

"What are you doin' out here, Frank?" Calloway asked.

"Why, I was just about to tell you that," Cooper said. "Nothin', nothin' at all. I've been looking for a job and haven't found a blessed thing."

85

Calloway and Galen looked at each other. "Why don't we take him to meet Slim? Maybe we can find him somethin' to do."

Galen magnanimously paid the check for their coffee, and they strolled along Hollywood Boulevard to Vine Street, then down a few blocks to Melrose, and then over to Gower Street, to the section then known in the film industry as Poverty Row. This was the area where the lower-class film producers, those who were trying to make movies on low budgets, had their offices. Many men who were later to become the most powerful figures in the film industry were working there then, doing business in one-room offices the size of telephone booths.

"Now, don't get your hopes up too high," Jimmy Calloway told Cooper as they walked along. "There's a good bit o' competition for these jobs. But Slim Talbot knows a lot of directors, and we make out pretty well."

Slim Talbot was standing on a corner, leaning against a telephone pole. He and Cooper greeted each other with hard digs in the ribs. "Well, boy, I'd say you growed some," Slim said.

"Frank wants to get into the movies, same as us," Jimmy Galen said.

"So that's it. Wal, don't get too steamed up. There's a chance . . . but we just have to be patient.

86

Now, I got some information today that they're makin' a Indian pitcher and they start pickin' out people today. It's called *The Vanishing American,* and a feller named Richard Dix is into it. He's a cowboy most of the time . . . in this one he's a Indian. They're goin' to need a passel o' riders, they tell me. We might get as much as a week's work. Maybe we'll just take a walk over there and see what we can see. . . ."

They did not walk; they rode in Slim Talbot's Model T Ford, bought with his rodeo winnings. At the studio, Cooper's spirits sank. There must have been forty cowboys clustered around the gate. Presently the casting director appeared. He was a small, chicken-like man with a pencil-line moustache. He gazed at the cowboy hopefuls as though they were so many head of cattle. "You'll do," he said to one. "You too, and you . . ." He hired Slim Talbot and six or seven other men—and then came to Cooper. He looked up at him incredulously.

"You're a cowboy?"

The old feeling of awkwardness suddenly flooded through Cooper's body, the same sensation of shame he felt so many times in school. He realized that he was the only man there who was not in cowboy clothes.

"You're the only cowboy I ever saw in a store-bought suit," the casting director said, scornfully, and began to move on.

Jimmy Calloway stepped in front of him. "Now, just a minute, Mister," he said. "You're lookin' at Frank Cooper, one o' the greatest riders ever to come out o' Helena, Montana."

"That's right, Mister," Jimmy Galen said, while Cooper listened in amazement. "This here rider makes all the rest of us look like tenderfeet."

The casting director looked at Cooper a second time. "Well . . . I'll admit he's *built* like a rider."

"What's the matter with a cowhand wearin' a suit and a necktie once in a while?" Galen demanded. "He's just on his way to see his . . . uh . . . girl."

Faced with this pressure, the director backed away. "Well, all right. What'd you say your name was?"

"Cooper."

"All right. Report tomorrow at nine A.M. That's all for today, fellows."

Calloway and Galen began whooping and dancing around Cooper.

"But . . . what about you guys?" he asked. "You didn't get jobs. He didn't pick you."

"Shucks, we already worked a couple days this week," Calloway said. "Friends ought to stick together, like. The more friends we got in this business, the more jobs we can hear about. Come on, let's get another cup o' coffee to celebrate. And, Coop, this one's on you. You're in the pictures now, Coop boy."

After they had their small celebration, Jimmy Galen took Cooper to an Army and Navy store, where they got him a pair of jeans and a cowboy shirt, complete with pearl buttons. Then they went down the street to another store, and the newly-hired cowboy extra picked himself out a ten-gallon hat.

"They look too new," Cooper said.

"Don't worry, we'll fix that," Galen said. "Let's go on home to your house."

An hour or so later, Mrs. Cooper looked out her kitchen window and saw her son behaving in a most peculiar manner. He and his friend were rubbing a pair of denim trousers into the dirt.

"Frank, whatever are you doing?" she called.

Cooper looked up, guiltily. "Oh, we're . . . ah . . ."

"We're just playin' a little joke on a friend, Mrs. Cooper," the quick-thinking Jimmy Galen said.

"It seems a strange sort of joke."

"Well, ma'am, he's such a dude, we thought we'd fix up his clothes a mite for him."

"Oh, you boys and your pranks," the mother said, fondly.

The next morning, Cooper got up before his mother and father were awake, put on his pre-dirtied clothes, and went out to Burbank, where the company was setting up for work. As soon as he arrived he found that all his diligent clothes-seasoning work of the previous afternoon had been for naught. Along with twenty-odd cowboys who had been hired for this sequence, he was issued a United States Cavalry uniform. The sleeves were too short and the breeches were too tight. "Never mind that," the unit director snapped. "You're not going to be in any close-ups, and the audience will never know the difference."

While the cameramen were getting their equipment in order, the director explained the scene. The Cavalry had been chasing a band of Indians for many miles, and now had them surrounded. "The first take will be a charge across the prairie, toward that tree over yonder. You'll start when I fire this gun. First man there gets an extra dollar—so go as fast as you can."

Cooper lined up with the rest of the troops. As far as he could see, he was the only man in a private's uniform. All the rest were wearing officer's insignia.

He patted his horse on the neck. It felt good to have a horse under him again, and he could hardly wait for the signal to gallop. It came before he was ready: *Crack!* went the director's gun, and the horsemen spurred their mounts into action. Cooper was taken by surprise. His horse reared and nearly threw him, but he held on, dug in his spurs, and soon caught up to the fleeing troops. They reined up at the tree in a cloud of dust, and from far away they heard the director cry, "Cut!"

Why, Cooper thought as they rode back to the camera location, this acting business is a cinch. Nothing to it.

A half-hour later he changed his mind. This time the troops were ordered to gallop into a grove of oak trees. It was a thick cluster, and the director insisted that his men had to ride directly into it. Cooper looked at the trees and their low-hanging branches and was about to protest, but thought better of it.

Crack! went the director's gun, and the men started off.

Just as he reached the trees, Cooper yanked on the horse's reins hard to stop him, but he was too late. A branch caught him by the shoulder and threw him off, and he narrowly missed being trampled by the onrushing horses behind him. He lay there, his face cut, his shoulder aching unbearably. Off in the distance he heard the director call, "Cut!" All around him he heard moans and groans. Some men actually had suffered broken arms and ribs. Nearly everybody had been hurt in some way; there were bodies all over the ground, and only a few of the troopers had managed to stay on their mounts.

"That was great!" the director cried as he ran up. "Very realistic, very true to life."

It was lunch time. Still feeling shaken, Cooper walked slowly to the commissary tent. He got his plate of pork and beans from the surly cook behind the serving table and went and sat down beside one of his fellow cowboy extras. The man nodded curtly and asked him where he was from. Cooper told him.

"First day?"

"Yup."

"You picked a bad one. It's not always this bad, but sometimes it's worse."

"What about those fellows who got hurt?" Cooper asked.

"Oh, they'll be back in action in a month or two. They always come back. Look at this." The man held out his right arm. It was as crooked as a forked branch. "Three breaks in that there. But you know, you can't beat the money. And it sure is better'n cow-punchin'."

They finished their beans and strolled out of the tent. The troopers—and some replacements for the injured—were beginning to assemble. Cooper felt someone pull at his sleeve. There was the director, a strange smile on his face. "You're Cooper?"

"That's right, sir."

"The casting department tells me they hear you're

a good trick rider. Somebody said you're the best that ever came out of Montana. That true?"

Cooper hesitated. "Well . . . I wouldn't say it myself, but I've been told I can. . . ."

"Good!" The director cut him off. "I need somebody to do a fall for me this afternoon. An easy fall from a horse—and he doesn't have to hit the ground with you. All you have to do is fall off. You can do that, can't you?"

"I reckon I can, sir."

"This is going to be *all your scene*," the director said. "You'll be *the star* of it."

"That's mighty nice," Cooper said, but he did not trust the man's smile.

His apprehension increased when he saw the horse he was to ride. The mount of the morning had been a good, reliable range horse, spirited but obedient. This one was an earthbound Pegasus. He was a stallion who did not like to be ridden, and he leaped and plunged when the budding actor finally got astride.

The scene called for Cooper to ride the horse at full gallop through a storm of arrows from the Indians. "Don't worry about it," the director called. "We've got expert archers here—they'll aim to miss you." Then he fired his blank pistol.

Cooper dug his heels into the horse, and they were off. Everything was going well, and he was in full

93

control, until the arrows began whizzing by. The horse reared and bolted, and Cooper lost control. From far off, he heard the director shout, "Hit the dirt!" It was a welcome cry; if it had not come, he would have jumped from the maddened horse just to get away from him. In amateur rodeos in Montana, he had learned how to fall from a galloping horse and had become proficient. All a rider had to do was let his weight fall on an outstretched arm, push with that arm, and roll on his shoulder, over on his back. He dived, putting out his arm—but the horse was going so fast his arm bent in two. He hit the ground with his shoulder, and his momentum carried him up, over, and around a second time, a double somersault that landed him on his head.

He lay there wondering if this was what death was like. The doctor rushed up, bent and poked at him. "Aw, shucks," the doctor said to the director. "Shook up a little, that's all. He's fakin'."

If Frank Cooper, a peaceable young man, had had the strength, he would have pulled himself to his feet and punched the doctor's nose. There was only one consolation. After fifteen minutes, they still had not caught the horse.

The director sauntered by to where Cooper was sitting, knees drawn up, head between them, trying to get his breath, wishing the pains would go away.

The horse bolted and Cooper lost control.

"Not bad," he said. "Maybe we can use you again sometime, Cooper."

The director would have had the same gift that Cooper had ready for the doctor; but he backed away, hastily. Eventually, Cooper pulled himself to his feet. He went over to the pay tent.

"Because you did a spill, you get ten dollars," the teller said. "Otherwise you'd only get five—first day's work, and all."

"Thanks a lot," Cooper said. But his sarcasm was lost on the man.

Never again, he told himself. Easy money was not worth that kind of punishment. Also, he had resented the casual, scornful way the director and everybody else had treated the cowboy extras. My first and last day in pictures, he thought.

But on the way home, he began to feel a little better. The smog that now covers Los Angeles in layers was not there then, and the air was clean and fresh. A few breaths, and somehow the bruises did not bother him as much as they had after the two spills. The ten dollars crackled in his pocket. Somewhere inside him a voice said that he had been nervous because it had been his first day. He had ridden worse horses in Montana. He had just not warmed up properly to that horse; given another day, he could take the spill in his own stride, not the horse's. He grinned at his own foolishness. The next time he would size up his horse first and then take his spill. All he could think of was: ten whole dollars! And for falling off a horse!

In that moment all thoughts of making a success of his art work drained from his head. Later there were to be lingering doubts, but for now all he could think of was that he seemed, at last, to have found something he could do. He rushed home to tell his father, and they had the conversation with which this narrative opens. Judge Cooper finally gave his consent; his son could try acting for a year. And from that point on, Frank Cooper was a movie actor. . . .

CHAPTER 7

POVERTY ROW

Young Frank Cooper soon learned that acting in films was more than a matter of getting on a horse and riding it, or sometimes falling off it, in front of a camera. To his astonishment, he learned that it was hard work.

The public seldom stops to think what the life of a film actor is like. Actors in their off-work moments generally are photographed at parties, skiing or water-skiing, hunting, fishing and the like. In order to get the leisure time to do these things, they must operate on schedules that would tire the hardest-working steelworker. The first call for an actor is usually at six A.M. He must go to the studio and be in the make-up department by six-thirty or seven. Being made up is sometimes an arduous process in itself; it can take as long as two or three hours, during which the actor must sit perfectly still while his face is refashioned. Then come at least eight, and often ten, hours of work during which he must not only exert himself physically but also must find in himself and express emotions that will be convincing on the screen. There are the lines to be learned, the other actors to adjust to, the costumes to be changed, and the occasional arguments with directors over the proper ways to play certain scenes. Sometimes there are temperamental actresses who insist upon having their own way or get sick in the middle of scenes. Tony Curtis has said that he nearly became a nervous wreck while making *Some Like It Hot* with Marilyn Monroe. There are always delays of one kind or another. Sets must be changed. Lights must be changed. A director may decide that one take, which already has been done a dozen times, must be done yet again and again. It is a rare day when an actor gets out of the studio at seven o'clock. After that he can go home, but generally he must spend his evenings learning more lines

medium was more effective and impressive in those distant days of the silents.

Cooper did not work in any major productions for many, many months, but almost from the beginning he worked steadily for the producers along Poverty Row. He became a member of a gang of cowboys, fugitives from rodeos and from the tough life of the range, who would hang around stables that rented horses to producers, hoping the latter would hire them as well as the animals. He and his friends were known as "corral buzzards." They had few periods of unemployment. Westerns were the most popular films being made along Poverty Row. A producer who knew his business could shoot one in between four and ten days. If he was trying something more ambitious, and had a little more money, the picture might take him as long as two weeks. First he would film the sequences involving the leading man, the leading lady, the villain and other people important to the plot. Then, on the last two or three days, he would call in a troupe of corral buzzards to give him his action. This mainly consisted of one group of men on horseback chasing another group. Usually the scenes were shot in limited areas of, say, no more than four or five acres. A resourceful director, by placing his camera at different positions around the lot and using his horsemen strategically, could make a chase staged in one of those small plots seem to take in many miles on the screen. Sometimes, in order to get as much use as possible out of the horsemen he hired by the day, a budget-conscious director would shoot more scenes than he needed and save the footage for future films.

"We never knew the names of any of the pictures we made," Cooper later recalled. "Sometimes, one day's work on location would turn up in three or four different pictures."

The more he worked in these quickies, as they were called, the more he was called upon to do. Falling off a horse was not enough. After a few weeks he was required to fall *with* the horse. The directors made horses fall by stretching a thin wire across the terrain to trip them, an inhumane trick that revolted Cooper. When he protested, one director said, "All right—if you can afford to hire a trained horse that'll fall on command, go ahead." From then on he refused to work for that director. Other cowboys had devised a method called the Running W. They would fasten a leather strap around one of the horse's ankles, with a wire running up to the saddle. At the proper moment, they would jerk the wire and the horse would obediently take a spill. This method also struck Cooper as cruel.

To avoid working in scenes requiring horses to take hazardous spills, he kept volunteering for scenes in which the only risk was one he would take himself. Many of the pictures featured fight scenes between the hero and the villain; the cowboy extras were used as doubles in these scenes. Cooper fought men in saloon sets, in stagecoaches and on top of them; he fought on the edges of steep cliffs and in the beds of rocky creeks and streams. He developed the technique of throwing a fierce punch but pulling back at the last minute, and he learned to fall to the ground with a crash as though knocked cold. In some scenes, he and his antagonist would use breakaway chairs made of light wood which would shatter convincingly when they hit each other with them.

In many ways, Cooper and his fellow corral buzzards were among the most important people in these early pictures, for the public went into the movie houses to see action—chases, fights, massacres, etc. Yet there was a caste system in Hollywood as rigid as that of a medieval court. The big stars did not speak to those just beneath them in order of importance. And nobody spoke to the corral buzzards. They were on the lowest level.

Nothing prevented Cooper from standing around while the actors were going through their scenes, and after a while he began to feel that he was learning something about acting. And almost before he knew it, he was beginning to think that some day he might like to try it himself. But every time he went to one of the directors he knew and applied for a part just above the corral buzzard class and just below the supporting actors, he was turned down. "You're too good a stunt man," they always said. "We need you for the action scenes."

It seemed to him that the physical demands were increasing. There was scarcely a scene in which he did not sustain a bad bruise or a severe cut. At nights he would ease into bed and sleep in odd positions to keep from irritating some tender spot on his body.

"Frank, why do you keep on with it?" his mother asked, over and over.

"Why, look at the money I'm saving," he would answer, proudly. He did not tell her, perhaps because he still was not quite certain about it, that his ambition to go to Chicago was fading. He still felt that the possibility of his ever becoming a real actor was remote, but at least it was a possibility. That kept him going.

One evening at dinner, Judge Cooper had some news. "I met an old friend of mine today," he said. "A lawyer. We got to discussing our children, and I told him about your being in the movies. What do you think? His daughter is in the pictures, too. I said we ought to get the two of you together. It would be nice if you knew somebody besides those riff-raff cowboys you're always around with."

Cooper's heart sank. There was nothing more depressing than the prospect of an arranged meeting staged by his parents and the girl's.

"It might help you some if you knew this girl," the Judge said. "Her name's Marilyn Mills."

Cooper dropped his fork. "*Marilyn Mills?*"

"That's it. Ever hear of her?"

Had he heard of her! Cooper laughed. "Marilyn Mills," he said, speaking to his father as though explaining something to a child, "is one of the most important people around the business right now. To begin with, she's an actress—but she's something else that no other girl is, too: she's a *producer*. She makes her own pictures. Why, she'd never even *look* at a corral buzzard."

Judge Cooper was unimpressed. "As far as I know, all she is to me is my friend's daughter. I said the two of you ought to get together, and he agreed. He said he'd tell her about you this evening. Here—" he finished, handing Frank a card, "this is her address. She'll be expecting you tomorrow."

"Father," said Cooper, "you just don't understand

about these things. I can't go to see Marilyn Mills and say, 'My father knows your father.' "

"Why not?"

"I don't know why you can't," Mrs. Cooper said.

It was impossible to communicate with them. He excused himself from the table and went to his room, where he lowered himself gingerly onto the bed. He felt both exasperated with and grateful to his father, but more the former than the latter. The poor old man didn't understand. Marilyn Mills! He had to laugh. There was about as much chance of his meeting her as there was of his meeting Gloria Swanson, one of the foremost stars.

He lay chuckling to himself at his father's foolishness. Gradually his quiet laughter subsided, and he began to think about it. The way things were in the caste system, nobody would even consider him for an acting part. Perhaps if he got *outside* the system, just for the space of a meeting . . .

That was it. Excitement began to stir in him, and waned as quickly as it had come. There was his face. At that moment his lip was swollen from a cut he had sustained the week before in a fall from a horse, and his right eye was black from a fight he had been in that afternoon. There had been fifteen men in the fight, all flailing viciously at each other, and in swinging at one man in front of him he had not seen a man at his side. The latter's elbow caught him hard in the eye, and after the stars had subsided a deep blue-black color had flowed in. He couldn't go to see Miss Mills looking like this. As this thought was formed, another came: Why not? After all, she was an actress. Perhaps the cut lip and the black eye would prove that he was an actor, too.

And so it did, although not quite in the way he hoped. Marilyn Mills, when he finally got in to see her the next morning, proved to be as practical as she was beautiful—and, Cooper saw at once, she certainly was beautiful. She was a slender blonde, wearing a man's shirt, open at the neck, and a pair of jodhpurs, but the male costume only emphasized her femininity. She greeted him from her desk in a room decorated with still pictures from films she had made. In a chair at her side sat her partner, J. Frank Glendon.

"My father tells me you've been working as a stunt man," she began, after the greetings.

"Well, I did have one small part," Cooper said. "In one Tom Mix picture, I caught Mr. Mix as he fell out of his saddle, hit by a bullet."

She laughed. "And with that training, you feel you're ready to act?"

Cooper could not decide if she were making fun

of him. He wished he had not come. "Well, I . . ."

"Apparently they've been working you hard," she said. "You did get those in a picture, didn't you?"

He touched his lip and eye self-consciously. "Yes, ma'am." He stood up. "Well, I just came in more or less to meet you, so I guess I'll be . . ."

"Wait a minute, we've hardly got to know each other," the girl said. "Frank and I are casting a film right now. We hope to start next week. We need a heavy . . . a villain. You certainly look the part."

J. Frank Glendon nodded in agreement.

"That's very kind of you, ma'am," Cooper said, "but it may be this lip and this eye'll heal by the time you start . . . and then I won't look that way."

She laughed again. "We have a very expert make-up department," she said. "One man . . . but he's a miracle worker." Her eyes narrowed and she focused on his face as though she were inspecting a piece of furniture. "Yes, Cooper, I think you'll do."

The door opened, and in came a tall, arrogant-looking man.

"Bruce," said Marilyn Mills, "here's our villain for next week's picture. His name is Frank Cooper. Mr. Cooper, this is Bruce Mills, our director."

Bruce Mills was the personification of the old-time director. His gestures and voice were both those of the ham actor. He took one look at Cooper and covered his eyes with his hand. Shaking his head, he moaned, "Oh, no! Oh, no, no, no, no!"

Cooper stood up, wondering what was wrong.

"Why, Bruce, what's the matter?" Marilyn Mills asked.

"No, no, no! He won't do! He simply will not do! He's too tall, too skinny, too—oh, he's too *everything!*" The director peeked out behind his covering hand, then hid his eyes again. "I simply cannot stand it."

Cooper's shyness gave way to a charge of anger. "Now, wait a minute, Mr. Director . . ."

Marilyn Mills stood up. "Bruce, you're making a spectacle of yourself. Glendon, here, and I have decided that he'll be just fine for the heavy, and . . ."

"I can't *bear* it!" the director groaned.

"Well, it's settled," the girl said, throwing a reassuring look toward Cooper. "He'll report on the set next week. He may be thin, but we'll get some padding for him. Glendon and I want him . . . and we're the producers." Her voice had become hard and decisive. "He'll report to you on Monday." She came out from behind her desk and held out her hand to Cooper. "Right, Mr. Cooper?"

"Right, ma'am."

Leaving the office, he felt dazed. Not only had he landed a real part . . . she had defended him! He ran home to tell the good news to his mother, and he could scarcely wait for his father to get home from the office that night. Judge Cooper took it calmly. "You see, son? I told you it might be a good idea to meet that girl."

The next day, Cooper went down to a theatrical supplier's house and bought himself a quantity of make-up: white powder, lipstick, and mascara. Many times, on the set between takes, he had watched the leading men make up their faces (only the more prosperous producers could afford make-up men in those days; the Poverty Row producers insisted that actors do their own faces).

Mrs. Alice Cooper was a better-than-fair amateur photographer. Even in Helena she had had her own darkroom, and she now agreed to take some pictures of her son so that he could practice emoting. First he smiled, then he frowned, then he scowled. She duly snapped the shutter as he tried each emotion, and then she took them into the darkroom to develop them. Cooper was crestfallen when he saw the results. The harder he had tried to get the proper expressions as she was taking the pictures, the funnier the finished photographs were. He shook his head sadly. "Looks like it just won't work . . . I don't seem to have what it takes to be an actor."

Mrs. Cooper studied the proofs. "Son, it looks to me as though you're trying too hard. The expressions on your face are funny because they're exaggerated. You seem to be *making* faces. You ought to try to feel inside what you're trying to express. Don't do it deliberately . . . just try to feel it."

They tried another set of pictures, then another. Gradually the expressions became more convincing.

. . . a long, looping right.

But Cooper still was not altogether sure that he could succeed in his first part, and the night before he was to report for work at Marilyn Mills' studio, he slept badly.

Dramatic acting proved to be almost as hazardous as action. In the first scene that was filmed that morning, Cooper, as the villain, was to stage a fight with J. Frank Glendon in a cabin, knock him down, then pick up Miss Mills and rush out the door.

"Action!" the director called.

Cooper and Glendon stood toe to toe, then grappled. Glendon threw Cooper to the floor while the girl stood in a corner, feigning terror. Cooper got up, set himself, and let go a punch toward Glendon's jaw. In his eagerness to make a good impression, he forgot to pull back his fist at the last split-second. The fist smashed into its mark, and Glendon's eyes glazed over, but only temporarily; a second later they were blazing, for the punch made him lose his temper. As Cooper was picking up Marilyn Mills, getting ready to rush to the door with her in his arms, Glendon leaped at him, grabbed him by the shoulder, whirled him around and hit him a long, looping, punishing right. Cooper saw it coming but could not duck. He felt the impact, but only for a second. As he dropped to the floor, he fell quietly asleep. . . .

His face was wet when he awoke. Someone had thrown a bucket of water on him. Above him was J. Frank Glendon, rubbing his fist, which was swollen. He helped Cooper to his feet. "Sorry," he said. "I lost my temper."

"I don't blame you," Cooper said. "I should have pulled my punch."

"It was wonderful!" Marilyn Mills said. "It'll make a wonderful scene!"

Cooper touched his jaw, and withdrew his hand quickly as the needles of pain leaped out. Maybe, he thought, I would be better off confining my acting to horse-falling. But simultaneously he started to grin. It seemed to him that he had become a real actor at last.

CHAPTER **8**

IN A CLOUD OF DUST

Boyishly, Cooper had thought that once he had made a break-through, everything would be easy. The part in *Tricks*, which was the name of the Marilyn Mills opus, would lead to other things. Why, it would only be a matter of a short time before all the producers in town—not just the Poverty Row people, but the big ones—would be asking for him.

A week, two weeks, a month went by after *Tricks* was released. There were no requests for his service. Resignedly, he went back to being a corral buzzard. It had been a fluke, he thought. He went to see Marilyn Mills. She had suspended production for a time to make pictures for well-established companies. There was nothing she could do for him. The meeting depressed him even more. He began to wonder if she had been lying when she congratulated him at the finish of the filming of *Tricks*.

At one of the horse corrals he ran into his old friend Slim Talbot and poured out his troubles. Talbot listened, rolling himself a cigarette from a small bag of tobacco. Presently he said, "I saw that *Tricks*, Coop, and I didn't think you were half bad. If I was you, I'd go and git me a screen test."

Talbot went on to explain that in his opinion the young man was ready to move on from Poverty Row —not only because he had some acting ability, but because the fly-by-night producers could not think of him except as a rider and action man.

"But nobody will give me a screen test," Cooper protested. "There must be two thousand guys my age out here tryin' to get into pictures. The producers have to beat 'em off with wagon tongues."

"Why don't you make your own test?" Talbot asked, quietly.

The cautious Cooper's first reaction was similar to that he had had when his father had suggested that he meet Marilyn Mills. And so was his second reaction. He had a little money saved. Why not? He began making inquiries. He could rent a horse for $10 a day. A vacant lot at the corner of 3rd Street and LaBrea could be used for $5. A fine-looking cowboy suit, complete with chaps, would cost another $10.

He approached a cameraman he knew and asked him how much he would charge. "Forty dollars per hour," the man said. "And in advance."

The man meant it. On the day agreed upon, he refused to load his camera until he had been paid. Cooper mounted his horse and galloped off about thirty yards. "Come ahead!" the cameraman called. Cooper galloped toward the camera as fast as the horse would go, and just before he reached it he pulled back on the reins. The horse reared on his hind legs, then came down on all fours. Cooper leaped from the saddle, jumped over a low fence, took off his hat and made a low bow to the camera.

"That's it," the cameraman said.

"You're only going to do it *once?*"

"What do you think I am, an amateur?" the man sneered. "What do you want for forty dollars? Come into my shop in the morning—I'll give you your lousy film clip. I'll even give you a look at it."

116

Cooper was at the office before the photographer arrived the next day. When the man finally came and, after grumbling a bit, set up his projector and ran the film through, it looked as though the sixty-five dollars had been invested for nothing. The film clip ran less than forty seconds, and as far as Cooper could see, the man had done a superb job of photographing a huge cloud of dust. Also, at the end, when he took off his hat and smiled—the sight made him shudder. He looked sick.

"If I were you, Mac, I'd try some other line of work," the photographer said, with a nasty smile. "You're never going to be an actor, if you ask me."

"I didn't ask," Cooper said. He took his tiny can of film and left. The sad truth was, the man probably was right. Still, he had come this far. He had to take the next step. Slim Talbot had told him to take his screen test to a friend of his, John Waters, at Paramount Pictures. Waters was the director of a series of Westerns based on books by the tremendously popular Zane Grey. "He's always looking for new talent," Talbot had said.

Cooper sat in Waters' office anteroom for more than two hours, glumly conscious of the ten or twelve others who were waiting along with him. From time to time a girl would come out, call a name, and the man would go inside. He would be out in less than fifteen minutes, looking dejected. The only thing that gave Cooper any hope was the fact that none of the others had film cans with them, which meant that he was the only one who had come with a test.

Presently his name was called. Knees unsteady, he

It seemed to take less than forty seconds.

rose and went into Waters' office. The producer was a brisk, genial man. Slim Talbot had told him about Cooper, he said, and any friend of Slim's was a friend of his. "So, you've brought a screen test, have you?

Well, let's have a look at it." He led the way through a rear door, and they walked across a studio street into a projection room. "Here, run this," Waters commanded, tossing the can to a projectionist.

Standing in the darkened room beside the producer, trying to answer his many questions about his

career on Poverty Row, Cooper could not recall a single previous time when he had been so nervous. Waters seemed a kind man. His interest was obviously genuine. But nothing could stop the sweat from gathering on Cooper's forehead, and when the film was run off—it seemed to take even less than forty seconds—he found that his shirt was soaking wet.

Waters did not say anything at first. Later, Cooper knew that he was struggling to keep from laughing. Finally the older man found his voice. "I . . . ah . . . couldn't see the end there too clearly," he said. "Did the horse throw you over that fence, or did you jump it yourself?"

"J—jumped," Cooper gulped.

"There was a lot of dust there," Waters said.

"Maybe—maybe if I went and did it over . . ."

"No, no, never mind doing that," Waters said. As he spoke, he sensed how nervous the young man was. "Look here, Cooper, don't look so blue. The test wasn't bad. . . ." He grinned and patted the dejected cowboy on the shoulder. "What I could see of you through the dust, that is. But you ride very well, and you move well too when you're on your feet. You ought to be making a name for yourself one of these days. Of course, I couldn't tell much about your acting ability . . . but acting is something you can learn. Go to the movies?"

"Every night, almost."

"Good. You ought to study the big stars. Watch

Rudolph Valentino, John Barrymore, Wallace Beery. Watch how they behave. If you want to get ahead in this business, you've got to study it . . . and you've got to study the best. There's no school can teach it. The movies themselves have got to be your school. But if you study hard, I think you might amount to something." He looked up at the tall figure and grinned again. "You've got the physical equipment, all right." He looked at his watch. "I've got to go. I've got more people waiting. I tell you what. There's nothing doing here right now. We've been having scenario trouble on our next Zane Grey picture, and it's going to take a while for us to work it out. We won't be back in production on our next picture for . . . oh, at least a month. Give me a call in about a month, and maybe I'll find something for you. I like your style, boy, and I'd like to help you."

Cooper walked off the Paramount lot feeling as though he had just been granted every wish he ever had made in his life. Waters' phrases kept echoing in his ears. By jingo, he thought, if he thinks I've got something, maybe others will too! A month wouldn't be long to wait . . . or would it? As he thought of pacing off the days, the idea of waiting that length of time seemed all but unendurable. Yet he had to wait;

there was no way out of it. He rushed over to the horse corral to look for Slim Talbot to tell him the good news.

The older man nodded paternally. "That's good news, all right. John Waters is one o' the most looked-up-to men in the whole business. But why do you have to wait? Why don't you take that test somewheres else and show it to 'em?"

Cooper was troubled. "But . . . would that be all right? What if Waters found out?"

Slim shook his head in mock despair. "I tell ya, Frank, sometimes I wonder if you still have your born brains. Did Waters put you under contract? Did he make any commitment to you? Until he does, you're your own free soul. Now, go to it." And Talbot gave him a stiff slap on the seat of his pants.

That evening at dinner, Judge Cooper seemed pleased to hear the news. "Slim is right, Frank," he said. "Waters made no promises to you. His encouragement ought to give you enough courage to go and sell your wares elsewhere."

Goldwyn Studios was the next fort the cowboy chose to attack. By 1925, Samuel Goldwyn was regarded as one of the pioneers in Hollywood. An immigrant from Poland at the age of eleven, he had been a glove salesman in Gloversville, New York, for a time, a vaudevillian, and finally a shoestring film producer. With Cecil B. DeMille and Jesse L. Lasky he had produced the first full-length film feature made in the United States, *The Squaw Man*, in 1913. In Hollywood he had gone through a number of alliances with other producers and finally had set up his own company. Goldwyn was already a millionaire many times over, and his studios were among the most magnificent in Hollywood.

Cooper was not to see the beautifully-appointed executive offices—not on his first day, at least. Curt, disinterested secretaries kept sending him from one office to the next. This went on all morning, and by two o'clock in the afternoon he was almost ready to give up. Nobody, it seemed, was remotely interested in seeing his screen test. Then one secretary, friendlier than the rest, suggested that he go to see the director, Henry King.

From the look of King's office, he was low on the executive scale at Goldwyn Studios. The director's base of operations consisted of two rooms in an attic divided by bristol board. There was no one there, not even a secretary. Cooper sat down to wait. Presently a man entered. He was about ten years older than Cooper, and the latter thought he might be a leading man. "What do you want?" he asked.

"I brought in a screen test," Cooper said, holding up the small can. "I was hopin' to get somebody to have a look at it, but I can't seem to find anybody. It's not very good . . . I shot it myself, but maybe . . ."

"My name's King," the man said. He took the can and shoved it into the pocket of his sports jacket. "Stick around if you want to—or come back tomorrow." And he went out.

Cooper could hardly believe his luck in getting to the man without going through a secretary—but then he thought of the crudeness of the test. I've got no right to be optimistic, he thought.

A secretary came in. She was as rude as all the rest had been. "To see Mr. King, you'll have to have an appointment," she said. "He's very busy. He's getting a production ready—*The Winning of Barbara Worth.*"

"But . . . he's already taken my screen test."

"Well, when he gives it back, you can make an appointment. No, better call—he won't be seeing anybody for about three months at least."

"Could you mail my test back to me?" Cooper asked, dispiritedly.

"Write your name on this card, and I'll see what I can do."

"Ma'am," he said, "it's the only proof I've got, and

it cost me sixty-five dollars. I sure would like to get it back."

"I can't promise anything."

Cooper bent and was about to write his name and address on the card when the door opened and Henry King bounded into the room. He clapped the young man on the back.

"What's your name?"

"Frank Cooper."

"Have you got an agent?"

"No, sir, reckon I haven't."

King handed him the can. "Just a little dusty, wouldn't you say?"

Despite his disappointment, Cooper had to smile. "Yup."

"Dusty," King repeated, "but not bad."

Cooper's mouth fell open.

"In fact," King said, "pretty good. You've got something, young man. I noticed something about you the minute I came in a while ago. And you certainly can ride—unless all that dust was deceiving my eyes. What else have you done?"

"I've been a corral buzzard. Well . . . had one small part, in a picture Marilyn Mills made. *Tricks*. Wasn't much." Cooper could hardly believe he was actually being interviewed by the director.

"You move well, dust or no dust," said King, smiling. "And if you move that way all the time, I can use you." He turned to the secretary. "Draw up the standard contract."

Cooper was absolutely certain he was going to faint.

"How will sixty-five dollars a week be, to start?" King was asking.

The words seemed to come from outer space. Cooper could not answer. He swallowed hard, his Adam's apple bobbing.

"If you can gulp like that, I can use the gulp, too," King said.

CHAPTER **9**

FINDING AN AGENT

One of the stars that Frank Cooper had admired
most was the impeccable, romantic, dashing English-
man, Ronald Colman. Long before John Waters of
Paramount had advised him to study the actors who
impressed him, he had been doing just that, and he
had been more struck by Colman than anyone else.
Getting a contract at Goldwyn Studios was thrilling
enough—but when he learned from Henry King that
The Winning of Barbara Worth was to star Ronald

Colman, he was overcome with joy. Then too, the glamorous Vilma Banky also was to be in the picture. Miss Banky was billed as "the most beautiful girl in the world."

Cooper's part was small, as he expected it to be, but it was big enough so that the audience would see his face fairly often. Colman was playing a man from the East who had gone west to build dams, and Cooper would be his messenger boy. A fairly well-known actor named Harold Goodwin had been signed to play Colman's rival for the hand of Miss Banky. The plot was not complicated. It was the sophistication of the East, played by Colman, against the rugged simplicity of the West, as portrayed by Goodwin, competing for the hand of Miss Banky.

Goodwin was a busy actor. When Henry King was ready to begin shooting *Barbara Worth*, Goodwin was still working in a film at Warner Brothers. Samuel Goldwyn then decreed that King should go ahead and shoot the scenes in which Goodwin would not appear. After those scenes were finished to King's satisfaction, he called Goodwin to report to work. Goodwin still was not finished at Warner's.

"How soon will you be finished?"

"Not for another week, I'm afraid."

King made his decision. He called in Cooper.

"You're about the same general size and configuration as Goodwin," he said. "There are some shots in which he appears at a distance. The audience won't be able to see the actor's face. Do you think you can double for him?"

"I'll try," Cooper said, nervously.

The scenes went off very well, King thought. A few days later he called Cooper in again and said, "It looks as though we're putting you into this picture little by little, Coop. How would you like to try some middle-distance scenes in Goodwin's place?"

"I'd like to . . . but, Mr. King, I don't look the least bit like Harold Goodwin, not even at a middle distance."

"We'll fix that," King said. "We'll put a lot of dirt and dust on your face, and we'll have you turn your head half-view, so they only see part of your face. The audience'll never know the difference."

The next day at seven A.M., King took Cooper out on the back lot and set him to running in a dusty field. Around and around he ran, and each time he passed King, the director splashed him in the face with a hose. He ran what seemed ten miles before the director was satisfied that he had reached the proper condition of exhaustion. Cooper could hardly stand, he was so fatigued. King led him onto the sound stage. The scene called for Cooper to stagger into camera range, stumble, and collapse. "Action!" King cried, giving Cooper a push. When the overhead lights hit him, Cooper fell without being told. Ronald Colman grabbed him just before he fainted away.

Samuel Goldwyn was watching. "Congratulations," he said to King. "That boy looks to me as though he has real talent."

Cooper raised his head. "I wasn't acting, Mr. Goldwyn."

"A great performance," Goldwyn insisted. "King, I want to see you in my office."

A half-hour later, while Cooper was still recuperating from his exhaustion, King came up to him and stuck out his hand. "Hello, actor."

Cooper raised himself on one elbow. "I'm sorry, Mr. King. I did my best."

"You certainly did—and the old man was impressed. We're not going to wait until Goodwin finishes at Warner's. You've got the part."

"I've . . . *what?*"

"You've got the part. You're playing Goodwin's role."

Cooper was silent for a full minute.

"What's the matter, boy?"

"I think I'll faint again."

The Winning of Barbara Worth

King laughed. "You'd better go talk to Ronald and get your scenes worked out. You've got an important one coming up, you know."

All through the preliminary scenes, Cooper had been in such awe of Colman that he had not been able to do more than nod in return when the great actor gave him a cheery "Hello, there!" each morning. Now he was momentarily unhinged by the prospect of speaking to the star. He approached Colman's dressing room timidly.

"Come in! Come in, old boy! I say, that was quite

131

a go-'round you had this morning! But you know, you did that fall very convincingly indeed. I was afraid I shouldn't be able to fetch you up."

Cooper found his voice lodged somewhere in the vicinity of his ribs. "Mr. Colman—sir—I was just talkin' to Mr. King, and . . . Mr. Goodwin isn't goin' to be with us after all. They want me to . . ."

"You're going to play the part? My word! I say, what jolly news! Splendid, splendid!"

Cooper looked even more miserable.

"What's the matter, old chap? You do look a bit faint. Still a bit off from that workout, what?"

"No . . . no, sir," Cooper said. "It's just that I . . . well, you know, this is my first picture. And playin' with *you*, Ronald *Colman*, it's . . ." He paused, then let all his worries come out in a rush. "I just don't want to let you down, sir. I'm afraid I'm not good enough to play with an actor like you."

Colman, the most generous and mannerly of men, threw back his head and laughed. "Look here, Cooper, you can't be serious!"

"But . . . sure, yes, I'm serious."

"My dear *boy*. You *are* very young, aren't you? I mean to say, what should you worry about? Look here: easy does it, lad. Forget the acting, concentrate on the scene. Actors don't make good actors; scenes do. Just remember what we're supposed to be doing

132

in there, and you'll be all right." He smiled. "Also, I have the distinct feeling that all you have to do is fall asleep on screen—and every woman in the audience is going to have her handkerchief at the ready. I believe you've got what it takes, Frank."

The scene called for Cooper to die in Colman's lap. Somehow, when King called "Action!" he managed to control his nervousness. He forgot the camera was there: he followed Colman's instructions and pretended to fall asleep.

"Great!" King called.

"Very good indeed!" Colman echoed.

Walking down Sunset Boulevard the next day, Cooper felt that the city was his. He had given himself a year to make a success in pictures. Less than seven months had gone by, and already he had become a featured player. He was not yet a star, but in his intoxicated joy he felt that that would be only a matter of time.

He found himself heading toward the horse corral to tell the good news to his buzzard friends. Slim Talbot and the Jimmys, Calloway and Galen, were as excited as he was, but they pretended to be sad.

"Now that he's a actor, we'll never see him again," Galen said.

"That's right," Calloway said. "He won't talk to the likes of us."

"Do you notice," Slim Talbot drawled, "his hat sets funny-like on his head? Looks to me like he's got some swellin' up there."

"Next thing we know, he'll be goin' to parties at Sam Goldwyn's house," Galen said.

"And Ronald Colman's," Calloway added.

"With his *agent*," Slim added, sarcastically.

"In a *suit*," Galen said.

"With a flower in his buttonhole," said Calloway.

"Wait a minute, now, you guys," Cooper said. "You all know dang well I'm never goin' to——"

Slim said, "*You* wait a minute, Frank. We're jokin' —but *have* you got yourself an agent?"

Cooper looked blank. "What's an agent?"

"You been in pictures for all this time, and you don't know what an agent is?" the older man said.

"Slim," Cooper said, in utter seriousness, "you know what I've been doin' in pictures. No. I don't know what an agent is. What's he do?"

Slim Talbot explained patiently that an agent was a man hired by an actor to negotiate with studios in his behalf. An agent, he said, talked money for an actor when a studio wanted the actor's services.

"You see the way they figure it out here," Slim said, "you can't blow your own horn as well as somebody else can. That's what an agent feller does for you. Say Mr. Goldwyn wants you for a part in his next picture. You've been makin' sixty-five dollars in *Barbara Worth*. You want more money. You can't go to Goldwyn an' say, 'Mr. Goldwyn, I want more money.' "

"Why not?" Cooper asked. "In other businesses, guys go and ask for raises all the time."

"The actin' business is different," Slim said, as though talking to a child. "You can't say to Goldwyn, 'I want more money because I'm handsome and have talent.' Or, 'I want more money because my fans go to your pictures to see me.' Specially not *you*, Frank—you couldn't say things like that. You'd get all redded up and fumble around and you'd probably wind up with ten dollars less than you were makin' before. No, sir. You got to have an agent."

"How do I find one?" Cooper asked.

"Turn over a stone somewhere," Jimmy Galen said, and he, Calloway and Talbot laughed uproariously.

"What's that mean?" Cooper said, bewildered.

Slim Talbot said, "An agent is the lowest form of human life. He's like a lizard or a snail—that's what actors think. They're always runnin' their agents down. They always talk about 'em as though they live under rocks an' such."

"Then why do they have to have them?" Cooper asked, reasonably enough.

"Well, boy, it's just one more of the goofy things that go on in this goofy world out here," Talbot said. "When you went into the movie business you got into one of the strangest industries you'll ever find anywhere. Look at it this way. These producers here are manufacturers. But what do they manufacture? They manufacture things that try to make people's dreams real. They give people a chance to forget their own lives and live other people's lives for a little while. While they're doin' that they seem to live lives themselves that ain't exactly real. Look at the houses you see around here. On one street you'll see an English thatch-roof farmhouse, right next to it an Italian villa, and right next to that a Swiss mountain house, and maybe even next to that a house like you might find in Morocco. The houses are pretendin' to be somethin' else, too. Understand?"

"No," Cooper said.

"Out here, you never call a spade a spade until somebody else does," Talbot said. "They don't advertise pictures by sayin', 'This is a good picture.' What they say is, 'This is the greatest picture ever made in all the years of the movie business.' They try to sell 'em that way. Same with an agent. He don't go into a producer and say, 'I got an actor named Frank Cooper, he plays his parts pretty good.' The agent goes in and says, 'This actor I work for, Frank

Cooper, is the greatest actor since the invention of the movin' picture camera.' Could you say that?"

"I wouldn't say that about myself."

"See?" said the two Jimmys, together.

"You need an agent," said Talbot.

"It doesn't sound quite honest," Cooper said.

"It ain't honesty, it's the show business," said Talbot.

He went on to say that he knew an agent who might be willing to "handle" Cooper's career. An agent, in return for his negotiations, took as his pay ten per cent of the actor's salary. Cooper went to see the agent Talbot had recommended the next day. He turned out to be a little man, busy on the telephone, breathless, bounding around his office like a fat little rubber ball. He spoke of producers by their first names: "Sam," "Jesse," and "Adolph." He spoke in figures that made Cooper's head feel light. Cooper decided that he didn't want to be associated with this fast-talking, totally insincere little man. He sneaked out of the office while the agent still was on the telephone, shouting at a director.

A few days later, the Goldwyn Studios called him back for some retakes. A few scenes in which he had appeared in middle-distance shots were to be made into close-ups.

"You looked just fine in the rough cut of the film,

Coop," Henry King said. "We thought we'd fatten up your part a little."

While they were working, Cooper asked King if he thought he needed an agent. King allowed that it might not do him any harm. "I think you've got a future," he said.

"If you think so," Cooper said, "then why do I need an agent? Why don't I just stick with you? After all, you and Mr. Goldwyn gave me my first break."

"I don't want to discourage you, Coop," said King, "but this is a very uncertain business. Suppose something should happen here? You and I might have an argument, or Mr. Goldwyn might all of a sudden change his mind about your ability—that could happen. Or suppose the public doesn't respond to you the way we think it's going to? An agent can help you get work in other places—work you might not be able to get for yourself. An agent could make excuses for you that you couldn't make. If you walked into a producer and said, 'I was bad in my last picture, but it wasn't my fault,' his natural inclination would be to think you were just giving him an alibi. On the other hand, if an agent walked in and gave him the same story, the producer might be willing to listen to reason. Agents can think up excuses much better than the rest of us can."

Cooper's sense of values was repelled by this admission of the dishonesty that permeated the industry, but he was somewhat reassured when King said, "Of course, you can make sure your agent only says what you want him to say. You don't have to encourage him to lie, if that's what's bothering you. After all, he works for you. A lot of agents out here don't understand that. They think they're the bosses. They're wrong. By and large, I would say you probably ought to have an agent—but you ought to keep an eye on him. They're all pretty slippery characters."

Cooper went to see a number of agents recommended by friends. Most of them were exactly like the one he had visited first. Then someone told him about an agent named Collins—who turned out, to his surprise, to be a girl. They had a number of talks, and the more he saw of her, the more he decided that she might be able to do a good job for him. For one thing, she was sincere. For another, beneath her gentle manner she seemed to have a shrewd bargaining sense. They shook hands, and once again he felt like a full-fledged actor.

Miss Collins, whose first name was Nan, did her best to get work for her new client. She called producers all over Hollywood, telling them all how good he had been in *The Winning of Barbara Worth*. All were dubious. They had never heard of Frank

Cooper, and they were not of a mind to take a chance on an actor who had appeared in only one film that had yet to be released. After about a week, she called Cooper and asked him to come to see her.

"It's not just that your first picture hasn't come out," she said. "In the past I've often sold actors who've never had any parts in films at all. It's something else that's keeping me from getting jobs."

"What is it?"

She drew a breath. "Your name."

"My what?"

"Your name. 'Frank Cooper.' Between you and me, it's too ordinary. Too common."

Cooper was astounded. "How do you mean?"

"It's not romantic enough."

"Well, ma'am, I reckon my parents weren't thinkin' of me as a romantic type when I was a baby." He thought she was joking.

"I'm serious, Frank."

"So am I."

"I've been thinking of names for you. My home state is Indiana . . . and there's a city in it called Gary. What would you think of 'Gary Cooper'?"

Cooper said, slowly, "Not very much, ma'am."

"Think about it. It's much more romantic-sounding than Frank."

He said it over to himself, "Gary Cooper."

"Frank Cooper just somehow sounds—well, too much like a farmer," she said, insistently.

"Gary Cooper. Don't know whether I like it or not. What about my middle name, 'James'?"

She made a grimace of dismissal. "James Cooper? James is the same as Frank. James isn't an actor's name, somehow. But . . . Gary! Think about it."

He thought about it. His astonishment at her suggestion now was compounded by his astonishment at finding that he liked the name. It *did* sound more like an actor's name, for some curious reason. The next day he called up Henry King at Goldwyn Studios and asked him to change his name from Frank to Gary in the cast of characters on his first picture. King agreed; they had not yet photographed the credits. From that day on, Frank James Cooper became known as Gary Cooper.

CHAPTER 10

TURNING POINT

In an industry growing as fast as Hollywood was in 1925, mix-ups were bound to occur. "Just when I thought I was riding high," Gary Cooper later told George Scullin, "I got lost in a wastebasket."

During the filming of *Barbara Worth*, Henry King had told Cooper that he might use him in his next picture. Some time after that, the astute Samuel Goldwyn mentioned something about putting the discovery under more or less permanent contract and suggested to Cooper that he see the casting director.

Cooper sent Nan Collins to see him. "The salary is sixty-five dollars a week," she said.

Cooper said, "Ma'am, I don't think that's enough. I think it ought to be seventy-five."

"They won't go up to that figure."

At this point he was operating on a cockiness that was due mainly to his youth. "Then I won't sign," he said, loftily.

"I think you ought to, Gary," Nan Collins said.

"No, ma'am. I think it ought to be more than that."

Nan Collins never went back to see the casting director. She knew it was useless. Perhaps if she had, Gary Cooper's career would have taken a different turn. He might have gone up faster, he later said, or he might have gone nowhere at all. The situation was roughly as follows, and it only could have happened in Hollywood when the industry was so young: Henry King thought that his superior, Samuel Goldwyn, had signed up Cooper; Samuel Goldwyn thought that his inferior, the casting director, had signed up Cooper. Cooper thought that neither Goldwyn nor King, nor for that matter the casting director, wanted him—because they had refused to meet his request for a ten-dollar-a-week raise. Nan Collins thought the whole thing was hopeless and, after making her original sales pitch to the casting director, had retired from the argument.

The result was that Cooper thought he was in demand, and the people at the Goldwyn Studios thought they already had demanded him. Nothing had happened. *Barbara Worth* had not been released; nobody in Hollywood knew that a new star

He waited to hear what his fate would be.

was about to be born. Cooper, by nature a retiring and reticent young man, stayed at home by the telephone, hoping to get a call telling him what his fate was to be.

The telephone did ring one day, but it was not the Goldwyn people calling. It was John Waters, the

144

Paramount man who had been the first to see his test. "You ought to stop by one of these days, Coop," Waters said. "It looks as though we might be able to find something to do with you."

One of these days, indeed! Cooper was there that afternoon.

"We finally got the script worked out for the new picture," Waters said. "It's Zane Grey's *Arizona Bound*. I saw a sneak preview of *Barbara Worth*, and I liked your performance. How would you like to have a try at the lead in this picture?"

Cooper gave a war whoop that would have been appropriate for one of the Indians he had played on the screen. "Wow! Would I!"

"I kind of figured you might say that," Waters said. "We go on location to Bryce Canyon, Utah, and because we've got a good budget, we'll be out there at least two weeks. Everything ought to go smoothly . . . we've got Thelma Todd for the leading lady."

Thelma Todd was tremendously popular with the public. She was known as "box office insurance": every picture she made was profitable for its producers. Playing opposite her, Cooper could be certain that he would have an audience for his first starring role.

Then, at Bryce Canyon, he was not so sure. He and Miss Todd got along very well off camera, but when

they had a scene together he became stiff and awkward. Scene after scene had to be rephotographed in
order to let him try to get some animation on his face.
"Don't worry about it," Waters kept saying, but he
worried more than he had at any previous point in
his life. He could not sleep at night; he reported for
work each morning looking worn out. Miss Todd
was sympathetic and helpful, trying to loosen him;
he could not thaw. "I was like an iron deer in scenes
with her," he later said.

To try to get reactions out of his star, Waters
would stand just beyond camera range, talking constantly, but Cooper had to admit that if it had not
been for the director's skill in the cutting and editing
room, his first big part might well have been his last.
He came off better in the fight scenes. The villain was
played by an actor named Jack Doherty, who was
determined to do his part as realistically as possible.
His first punch shook loose a couple of Cooper's
teeth, whereupon the new leading man retaliated with
a blow so hard it nearly dislocated his arm.

Finally the film was finished. Cooper returned to
Hollywood with a distinct feeling of uncertainty. He
was not worried about the fights or the riding scenes.
In those he had been himself. But he felt certain that
once Waters and his superiors saw him in the love
scenes with Miss Todd they would decide they had

made a mistake. As he saw it, he had only one choice: to get another part as soon as he could before *Arizona Bound* was released and try to do better in that one. Then, to his surprise, Waters telephoned and said he was planning to use him in his next film, *Nevada*.

"But, Johnny, between you and me—I wasn't very good in *Arizona Bound*, was I?"

"Kid," said Waters, "you need experience. But a lot of experienced actors don't have whatever it is that you have. Some magnetic quality comes down off that screen and gets to people. I don't know what it is, but whatever it is, you've got it. Mark my word: one of these days you're going to wake up and find you're a big star. Just keep working at it, that's all."

The Paramount executives saw the rough cut of *Arizona Bound*. They agreed with Waters and decided to gamble on young Gary Cooper. In reality, it was not much of a gamble. They too were paying him only sixty-five dollars a week, and by putting him in pictures with stars who already were established they could make certain that even if he turned in a bad performance the picture still would earn money.

Nevada turned out to be better than *Arizona Bound*. Then the pioneering director William Wellman put Cooper in *Wings*, a film about fliers in World War I, with such well-known actors as

Richard Arlen and Charles "Buddy" Rogers. Clara Bow, later to become one of the most sensationally successful stars of the 1920's, also was in the movie. She was impressed by Cooper and asked that he be given a part in *It*, which was to be her most famous picture. Cooper also had a role in the next Clara Bow picture, a bigger part that did a good deal for him. By then he was earning $200 a week.

This second Clara Bow picture nearly proved a disaster for Cooper. There was a scene in which he was meant to enter a huge room filled with people in various stages of intoxication, and to make his way across, stopping here and there to take a drink from glasses held out by pretty girls. The scene revolted him; something kept him from doing it as the director wished. According to the Hollywood columnist Hedda Hopper, who was then an actress, he had to do the scene no fewer than twenty-two times before a passable take could be made. Even then the final scene was dreadful. Cooper fled the lot. He was so dejected he could not bring himself to go home. It seemed that he would never be an actor. He walked and walked, all night long, and eventually wound up on the beach at Malibu, north of Hollywood. There he sat down and, staring out over the ocean, began to think about himself. It seemed to him that he had been a victim of self-delusion of the worst kind. He would never be an actor; he was sure of that. Every time he had to do something that was not in keeping with his real character, he looked clumsy. Also, the face he saw on the screen was not really his. It was so covered with thick make-up he looked like a circus clown. All at once he realized that he hated the whole business. This was not so, but he was using "the business" to conceal his sense of inferiority. He came to a decision. He would walk into the studio the next day and announce that he was quitting the picture. He would get another job, and eventually, perhaps, he would go back to his original plan and go to art school. He walked back home, his mind made up.

He slept until nearly noon the next day, then went to the studio. Instead of going in at once, he went to a nearby restaurant and had a cup of coffee. He was still sitting there a half-hour later when Frank Lloyd, the director, found him.

"Miss Bow sent me to look for you," Lloyd said. "She says you must not be discouraged. That kind of scene just isn't your style. You'll do better in the others."

"I doubt it," Cooper said. "I'm just not the drunken-party type, I guess. I'm more an action type."

"She'll coach you herself," Lloyd said. "And I'll do what I can in the cutting room. You'll get through, Coop."

"Get through" was an understatement. During the

next five years, Cooper became one of the most popular actors in Hollywood. He was able to make the transition to talking pictures without difficulty; some of his contemporaries found their careers were over when the films required them to talk, but his voice came through the theatre loudspeakers pleasingly. The real turning point in his career came with *The Virginian*, made in 1929, the first big outdoor talking picture.

"After *The Virginian*," Cooper told the reporter Leonard Slater in 1961, "I got so busy that I was making one picture in the daytime and another at night. After a day's work, I'd shave, change clothes, have dinner and work until my eyes began to cross . . .

"My weight went from one hundred eighty to one forty-eight. I didn't have an ounce of flesh to spare. It was true that I was earning four hundred dollars a week . . . had fan clubs, and got my name in the newspapers; but I was so tired and depressed that I wanted to give it all up. I found I was suffering from exhaustion and jaundice.

"The studio gave me five weeks' vacation, so I dug into my savings and bought a trip abroad. I needed some time to recover my health and find out what I was doing wrong . . ."

Even at this point, he still was not certain of his

First he went to Algiers.

talent. He believed that only his energy had carried him along in films.

He went first to Algiers, where he was surprised, upon first setting foot on the dock, to find little boys dancing around him, pointing their fingers like guns, shouting, "Boom! Boom!" They made him feel better: "At least I'd impressed somebody in the world," he told Slater. From Algiers he went to Venice, where he decided to stay for a while and rest on the Lido Beach. Soon after that he had a cable from Walter Wanger, the production chief at Paramount, urging him to get in touch with the Countess Dorothy DiFrasso, an American woman who had married a member of the Italian nobility. She had a house in Rome, Wanger's cable said.

Cooper went on to Rome, where the Countess welcomed him and made him a member of her set. For five weeks he lived in what amounted to a continuous party, meeting members of the nobility, internationally-known playboys and glamour girls, millionaires and soldiers of fortune. He enjoyed himself, most of the time, but at the same time he felt—as usual—out of place. "I'm afraid the old saying applied to me," he later said. "They could take the boy out of Montana . . . but they couldn't take Montana out of the boy." He was glad to get back to the United States.

As soon as he arrived, the studio set him to work

with Claudette Colbert in *His Woman*. He had not been working for three weeks before he began to feel terrible all over again—and this time he seemed to be worse than he had been before his vacation.

The studio doctor examined him, then called him back the next day and gave him his report. "Coop, you're anemic," he said. "You're so low in that blood count of yours it's a miracle you're able to walk around. You're still suffering from jaundice. My recommendation is that you take six months off. No partying. You *rest*."

At the Countess DiFrasso's house in Italy, Cooper had met a man named Jerome Preston who owned a huge ranch in Tanganyika. Preston had invited him to visit there several times, and he now accepted the invitation. It was only when he arrived that he realized how weary he was, and how sick. For weeks he simply lay in a hammock on the veranda of the ranch house, gazing through binoculars at the wild antelope grazing in the distance. Gradually he began to feel better. Preston had some fine Arabian horses, and Cooper took to riding out on the vast plains just to watch the animals. One day he saw twelve different species of antelope. Another time, as he was watching a huge herd of nyala, he saw a lion charge out of the bush, spring upon a buck, bring it down, and proceed to make a meal of it.

Jerome Preston had been in Europe. When he returned he brought with him the Countess DiFrasso and a huge party. Somewhat to Cooper's alarm, the high living began all over again. The Countess insisted upon organizing a safari to go for big game on the slopes of Mt. Kenya. "With Preston acting as organizer, we assembled enough cars, trucks, camping gear and luxury items to support a regiment," Cooper once told George Scullin.

The newspapers in the United States made sport of the expedition, especially when it was learned that the Countess insisted that everyone in her party dress for dinner while in the bush. Again Cooper felt out of place. Later, when the huge party left Africa and went on to the various resorts around the Mediterranean—Monte Carlo, Cannes, Antibes, Nice—its gaiety becoming more and more abandoned with each stop, he gradually came to the conclusion that he had better get back to Hollywood as soon as possible. He was not sure yet that he was really a movie star, but he knew one thing with certainty: he never had been meant to be a playboy.

CHAPTER **11**

"WHO IS THAT GIRL?"

It was one of those fabulous, crowded, glitteringly expensive parties that were common in Hollywood during the 1930's. The country was in the grip of the great depression that began after the stock market crash of 1929, and everywhere people were jobless, homeless, and hopeless. Yet Hollywood continued to prosper—perhaps because it was selling hope and glamour, romance and adventure, and people were willing to spend their last dimes to go into theatres and get their minds off the hard times out-side. Hollywood gave them the dreams they needed to face reality.

This party was given by Cedric Gibbons, perhaps the most famous art director in the film colony, and his wife, the exotic Mexican actress Dolores del Rio. Gibbons had done the art direction for a film Cooper had made, *Today We Live*. During that time Cooper had told him that he once had hoped to be an artist. Gibbons had laughed at the idea of an *actor* wanting to be an artist. The two men had become good friends —but what Cooper did not know was that the older man had invited him to this party because he had been asked to invite him.

Cooper stepped into the wide parlor, filled with chattering, expensively-gowned and bejeweled women, their escorts all in tailcoats and white ties. An orchestra played in the background. Red-jacketed waiters moved here and there with trays, and at one end of the room an elaborate buffet was set up. The young man from Montana could not help thinking, as he always did when he attended one of these dream-world functions, that it was like a scene from the movies. He looked around the room. Nearly every face would have been recognizable to all the movie-goers of America. This was, indeed, the Hollywood elite—and, as he had done so many times, he began to wonder how it had happened that he was a part of it. Why, he wondered, did it happen to me? His internal musings quickly came to a halt.

Across the room was the prettiest girl he ever had seen in his life.

He looked at her a second time, and decided he was wrong. She was not the prettiest girl he had ever seen in his life. She was the most beautiful young woman he had ever seen—so beautiful that he felt his huge frame begin to shake a little, as it did sometimes when he was about to play a scene that was important to him. For he realized at once that something very, very important was happening to him.

This was the summer of 1933. When he had returned from Africa, broke, wondering if he had a future in the film business, he had found to his astonishment that he had become one of the most sought-after actors in Hollywood. His pictures had made huge sums of money. His fan mail was being carried in by the truckload. Exhibitors were sending urgent wires: WHEN DO WE GET A NEW GARY COOPER PICTURE? He was regarded as so important to the industry that, when it seemed possible that he might not come back, they had found another young man they hoped might take his place and had given him a similar first name. The young man's real name was Archie Leach; they called him Cary Grant.

As soon as Cooper had come back, he was put to work in bigger and bigger parts in one film after another, cast and executed by the best in Hollywood. His leading ladies were among the most famous in the business. They brought Helen Hayes, who had made her reputation on Broadway, out to star with him in *A Farewell to Arms*, the adaptation of Hemingway's modern classic. In rapid succession he made *Today We Live*, *If I Had a Million*, *One Sunday Afternoon*, and *Design For Living*, the latter with Frederic March and Miriam Hopkins. His salary was now $6,000 a week. He had a custom-made Duesenberg sports roadster "so long I had to start turning corners in the middle of the block," a well-appointed apartment, and a gun collection second to no other Hollywood hunter's. When he felt like hunting or fishing, he went with his friends. When he felt like riding, he rode. His life was about as pleasant and diverting as any young man's ever could be—for in addition to all the items listed above, there was also a large and ever-growing collection of dazzling girls who were pleased to go out with him in the evenings.

Yet, he did not go out much. He never had been particularly interested in girls. In college he had made dates for proms and parties, but not out of any deep desire for the company of females; he did it more because all his friends were doing it. The fact is he was

158

still as shy as he had been in Montana. He was still
conscious of his tallness, and somehow whenever
he was on a date it did not seem right to him to tell
the girl about a grouse he had bagged on a hunting
trip the week before. For some reason girls were not
as interested in those things as he was. Nor could he
discuss carburetors, or the relative merits of wire or
disc wheels. On the screen he often played a man who
was inclined to scuff his foot and become tongue-
tied in the presence of a lady. Those parts came
easiest to him because in those years that was essen-
tially how he was. In Hollywood his name frequently
was mentioned in gossip columns in connection with
some of his leading ladies. For a time it was said that
he was in love with Clara Bow; then with Lupe Velez,
the Mexican star; then with Tallulah Bankhead; and,
for a time, with Evelyn Brent. After that it was said
that Countess Dorothy DiFrasso was his main interest. All these reports were fabricated by press
agents who felt it necessary to make their cowboy
seem a more romantic figure to his public. He never
had dated any girl more than three times at the most.

Now, at the sight of this girl across the room,
genuine interest in a member of the opposite sex not
only stirred in him, but, as he later expressed it,
"socked me right on the jaw."

He made his way through the crowd until he came

159

to his friend Gibbons, who was talking to some producers.

"Cedric, who is that girl over there?" he demanded, plucking at the art director's elbow.

Gibbons turned away and glanced briefly in her direction. "Oh, her. My niece." He turned back to his conversation.

Cooper stared at the girl again, hoping to catch her eye. She was talking to someone else and did not look his way. He grabbed at Gibbons' sleeve again. "Ah, uh, Cedric," he said.

"Gary, what's the matter with you?" Gibbons said, in pretended irritation.

"I, uh, would like to meet that girl." He swallowed. He felt odd.

"Oh, all right," Gibbons said, as though exasperated. "Come on." He reluctantly began to propel Cooper across the room.

"Wait a minute, pardner," Cooper said. "Tell me a little about her."

Gibbons rapidly sketched the girl's background. She was from the East. Her stepfather was Paul Shields, the noted yachtsman, a member of the board of governors of the New York Stock Exchange, a Social Registerite.

"Social . . . Register?" Cooper asked, falteringly.

"Her grandfather was Harry Balfe, the millionaire," Gibbons said, as though trying to blurt out everything and get on to something more interesting. "She's just out of school."

Social Register, Cooper was thinking glumly. Well, that does me in. What does a cowboy say to a lady?

Then, suddenly, he brightened. On safari with the Countess DiFrasso's party he had met any number of excessively social people, including some titled Europeans. He had hunted with them and gone to their parties. Perhaps this girl might know some of the same people; they would have that in common to talk about.

When he looked into the girl's eyes he found all his opening remarks running out of his head. He was as stiff and fumbling as any character he had ever played—perhaps more so, for this meant so much more to him.

"Miss Veronica Balfe, this is Gary Cooper," Cedric Gibbons was saying.

Her clear blue eyes stared hard at him—in something close to contempt, he thought in panic.

"I know," she said. Her voice sounded cold.

Cooper wondered whether he was meant to be flattered or ashamed. She had a low, penetrating voice; he had never heard a voice like that before. He did not know then that she had seen him while she was a student at the Bennett School for Girls, at Millbrook, New York. A theatre near the school had played Marlene Dietrich's first American film,

Morocco. Although Cooper was her leading man, he and the most important supporting actor, Adolphe Menjou, were scarcely mentioned in the advertisements. Miss Dietrich had been a sensation in Europe, and the studio press agents were determined to make her one in America. Yet the schoolgirl had been so struck by the actor that she waited until the film began again, so that she could see his name in the cast of characters. When she had come to Hollywood to visit her Uncle Cedric, she had asked if she might meet him.

Now that she was face to face with him, she was nearly as shy as he. She covered her feelings by pretending to be fully in command of herself.

He was saying something inane, something straight out of a Gary Cooper picture: "Ma'am, you're pretty enough to be in pictures."

"That's no great accomplishment," she said.

He blushed. "Well, I . . . ah . . . meant that—" He could not go on.

"Rocky's *been* in pictures," Cedric Gibbons said.

It was true. One of the reasons she had come out on the visit was that her drama teacher at Bennett had told her that she had real talent as an actress. At a party at Gibbons' house she had met David O. Selznick, the producer. Today Mrs. Cooper says, "The less said about my acting career, the better. When I met Mr. Selznick I was signed up before I quite knew what was happening. I had no talent whatsoever. They called me Sandra Shaw . . . or Sandy . . . or Stormy Weather, or something. I did two pictures, both now forgotten, fortunately."

Miss Shaw-Balfe confessed to the big young man before her that she was also in the movies, as her Uncle had just said, but she hastened to add, "I know I'm able to do something, but I don't think acting is it."

Somewhat to his own surprise, this came as a relief to Gary Cooper. Without understanding why, he had experienced a flash of alarm when Gibbons had said the girl was an actress. He actually had thought, "One star in the family is enough." As he stared at her and considered this thought, he wondered how it had come into his mind. He tried to think of something else to say to conceal the storm of confusing thoughts that were running through his head.

She saved him. "I saw you in *Morocco*," she said. She did not tell, not just then, that she had waited to find out his name, nor that she had asked to meet him.

Cooper muttered something that might have been, "Oh, that wasn't much. That was Miss Dietrich's picture . . ."

"I thought you were very good," she said. "How did you get into movies, anyhow?"

Cooper seized this opportunity. This was a safe subject: his career. If he could talk about that, perhaps she would not notice how she was affecting him. He began to tell her, beginning with the days when most of his acting had consisted of falling off horses. He was astonished at his own verbosity. Why, this was the easiest girl in the world to talk to, this debutante from the East. He talked on and on—and was still talking when the other guests were saying good night. This was the first known instance of what later was regarded in Hollywood as a phenomenon. Cooper, with nearly everyone else, was taciturn, reticent, and given to one-syllable comments and answers. Silence, punctuated by "Yups," became his trademark. Reporters went to him for interviews, spent hours asking questions, and realized that he had said so little they had practically no notes when they went away. On hunting trips with friends he talked normally; it was as though the familiar outdoors could loosen whatever it was that blocked his speech. But usually he was a non-talker . . . except with Veronica. For a reason that neither could ever explain, she acted as a catalyst. In her presence he seemed to make up for all his previous silences.

They said good night. Cooper telephoned her at Gibbons' house the next day. She was out. He tried the day after that. Still out. Days went by, and she always was out; he began to think that he never would see her again. The thought upset him and brought on anger. He called up Gibbons. "Darn it, Cedric, why can't I see that niece of yours?"

"Well, she's a very popular girl," Gibbons said, teasingly. "Very busy . . ."

Then he told Cooper there was a boat trip planned for the following Sunday to Catalina Island. "Would you like to go?"

"Oh, boy!" Cooper shouted.

He could hardly wait until Sunday, but meanwhile he admonished himself to get control of his emotions. After all, he had only seen this girl once, and then only for the space of a few hours. She had not said much; ruefully he admitted that he had not given her a chance. Even though she had seemed a steady, intelligent, even-tempered girl (as well as the loveliest he ever had seen), it was just possible that she was like all Social Registerites he had heard of—scatterbrained, dedicated to pleasure and nothing else, a butterfly. He would be calm and contained about the whole thing, he decided.

One sight of her on the boat wrecked all his schemes. He went over to her and, without preliminaries, said, "Doggone it, Miss Balfe, I've been calling you for days. Why won't you go out with me?"

"Who says I won't?"

From that point on, Miss Veronica Balfe's calendar

They were happiest when they were outdoors.

remained crowded—but virtually the only name on it was that of Mr. Gary Cooper. They went for long drives up the Pacific Coast highway, stopping for dinner at little inns where Cooper was reasonably sure he wouldn't be recognized—not because he wanted to keep his romance a secret, but because he did not want to be bothered by fans when he was out with his girl. They went to swimming parties at friends' houses, they went on yacht trips. Sometimes they would drive up into the Hollywood Hills and park at night, looking down on the sparkling colored lights of the city. They talked endlessly. She told him about her girlhood, and he filled in more stories of the ranch days and his early struggles in pictures. They discovered that they both were happiest when they were outdoors; she loved to ski and go sailing, and she was sure she would enjoy going along on hunting trips with him, although she wasn't certain that she would enjoy firing a rifle.

Before they quite knew what was happening, it automatically was decided. "How do you like that house?" he would ask as they passed one that struck his fancy.

"No," she would say. "It looks too much like Hollywood—all that mixed-up architecture."

They must have looked at two dozen before they found one they liked. It was located in the San Fer-

nando Valley, and was a squarish, simple-lined structure surrounded by ten acres of land. Cooper signed
a lease almost at once. They went home to break the
happy news to the Gibbonses, who had expected it
and were overjoyed. Then Rocky—Gary had begun
to call her by that nickname because it struck him as
funny for a girl so fragile—called her mother and
step-father to tell them.

They were shocked. "Marry *a movie star?*" her
mother cried. "And that one?"

She had read the reports the press agents had put
in the gossip columns. She imagined that Gary Cooper
was the personification of the Hollywood wolf.

"But, Mother—"

"Veronica, you come right home! Come home at
once and get this foolishness out of your head!"

In tears, the girl appealed to her uncle. Gibbons
grabbed the telephone. "Now, look here!" he cried.
"This man is my friend! Furthermore, he's one of the
nicest guys I've ever met in my life! Furthermore,
he and Rocky are in love and want to get married!
Furthermore, *I* approve of it. She couldn't find anybody half as good in the East, not even if she married
a *Yale* man!" And he went on like that. Mrs. Shields
retreated.

Frank James Cooper and Veronica Balfe were
married in New York on December 15, 1933. They
moved into the house in Van Nuys. On September

15, 1937, their only child, Maria Veronica Balfe Cooper, was born. For twenty-four years the three Coopers lived one of the happiest existences of any family in Hollywood. They did everything together from the time Maria was able to walk—they skied in Colorado and in Europe, summered in Southampton and sometimes wintered in Florida, went to Europe on extended tours, and, when they were home in Hollywood, lived a quiet family life that was very much removed from that of the rest of the film colony. They had only a few close friends; they seldom went out. Mrs. Cooper devoted herself to charities, and so did Maria when she was older. Both were devout and active members of the Catholic Church. From about the time of the marriage on, Cooper's career climbed and climbed until his place on the list of the ten top box-office drawing-cards was unshakably secure. He made one success after another, won two Oscars, and gained the reputation as perhaps the most reliable of all the actors in the business. In his late fifties he was still playing the parts of men much younger, and playing them so well that his millions of fans began to think of him as ageless. It pleased those fans to think of this tall American as he was—a diligent, successful human being who lived a happy, serene, exemplary family life. Thus, when he was stricken by cancer, the world went into mourning.

CHAPTER **12**

A NEED FOR FAITH

It was, James Stewart later said, the hardest task of his life. Gary Cooper was his close friend. He had met his bride in Cooper's house. They had gone hunting together, they had had long, intimate talks on subjects important to them. The Academy of Motion Picture Arts and Sciences had voted to give the dying Cooper a special award, and Stewart had been chosen to make the speech of acceptance. At the ceremonies on the night of April 17, 1961, Stewart found it hard to keep from weeping as he stood before the television cameras and said, "We're all very proud of you, Coop. All of us are tremendously proud . . ." He stepped down, quickly, to keep back the tears.

In an article written in May, 1960, Thomas B. Morgan had set down a list of mishaps and ailments Gary Cooper suffered over the years of his career: first, of course, there had been the cracked hip in the accident with Harvey Markham, back in Helena. Then had come the innumerable spills in his early days of films, in one of which he had damaged his right arm so badly he could not lift it above his head. Following that he had had the attack of jaundice that had sent him to Africa. Morgan continued, "He developed an ulcer after he had made *High Noon,* and last year he had been in surgery twice within six weeks for internal troubles. In addition, he'd had four hernias besides all the minor accidents connected with movie-making: pinned underwater and almost drowned; cut by falling debris after a bridge explosion; hearing impaired in the left ear by a dynamite blast; wrist-sprain, cut lip, and black eye suffered when a brother actor had become too realistic in a fight scene; left shoulder wounded by a blank pistol fired at close range by Burt Lancaster; and hands burned putting out a fire in his dressing room on the set of *The Naked Edge.*" Cooper once had told Louella O. Parsons, "All my life I've been held to-

just went to church when Sunday came, without questioning, without making any fuss."

Young Cooper would grow restless during the services as boys so often do. He wished he could be out walking the range with his gun and one of the dogs, or riding his horse with his Indian friends.

All his life he seemed to require long periods of solitude, from which he would emerge fresh and seemingly rejuvenated. It may be that during these periods he gradually was growing closer and closer to genuine belief. His friends all noticed that as he grew older he became more thoughtful; often, in the middle of conversations, he would grow silent for moments at a time, as though searching himself.

His mother later said that she believed that his acceptance of God came about through the example of Rocky, his wife. And the wife, in turn, always believed it was the example of the daughter, Maria. The latter had gone to school at Marymount, in the Brentwood–Bel Air area. She had been one of those who accepted her religion from birth, and it had always been a source of deep comfort and inspiration. Perhaps the contemplation of his daughter's serene beauty, rooted in inner faith that almost seemed to glow on her young face, was what ultimately convinced Cooper that there would be something in the acceptance of faith for him.

173

He talked to a priest several times.

At one point in their adult lives, the Coopers found themselves quarreling more often than couples normally do. This sometimes happens, of course, in the most loving families. After talking over their increasing tendency to bicker, the two of them decided that it was decidedly harmful to their child. She could not help but be disturbed. They concluded that it would be best for them to live apart for a time. Cooper thereupon packed a few belongings and moved out of the house. The very next day he was back for a visit.

He continued to visit the house at regular intervals—there was scarcely a day when he did not turn up. Nor did he carry off any of the pictures, souvenirs, guns or other small possessions that were dear to him. It is not generally known, but during this short period he went to see a priest several times. There had never been any question of a divorce. Both he and Rocky knew that this was only a temporary period that they had to live through. "Perhaps if we had been stronger people the separation never would have occurred," Rocky said. "We were not that strong. Nobody is one hundred per cent perfect—except One. I prayed that we would be back together again, and my prayers were answered. He came back to the house."

The separation had lasted a year and a half. In the days just before he died, Cooper remarked more than once that he detested himself for that year and a half. Yet, Mrs. Cooper avers today, the separation actually had the effect of making the next ten years together much better, for as soon as they were reunited they dedicated their union to God by taking their marriage vows in a Catholic church, the Church of the Good Shepherd in Beverly Hills, in the presence of a priest.

Yet Cooper still was not quite ready to dedicate himself wholly to the faith. The processes of thought and emotion that brought this about will never be known, for he never spoke of them even to his wife and child. The many discussions he had with priests must have had a profound effect upon him, but he was not quite ready. Each Sunday morning he would see his two women, their faces radiant as they would pull on their white gloves, getting ready to go off to Mass.

"Don't you want to come along?" Rocky would say.

"Oh, Father, do come along," Maria would say.

"Well, I've got a few things to do around here . . ." Cooper would say, slowly, looking down at his feet. The only times he joined them were for services on Palm Sunday, Easter and Christmas.

To Rocky and Maria, his decision came suddenly, without warning. One bright Sunday morning as they were going out the front door, they heard him call from his dressing room, "Hey—wait for me." From then on he went regularly to Mass, and a short time later, after taking instruction, he was baptized a Catholic. That was in the latter part of 1959.

There are some people in Hollywood today who believe that Cooper's baptism approached the miraculous; that somehow he knew he would need an extra reserve of faith and strength to call upon in the days ahead. For it was not long afterward that his health began to fail.

Early in 1960, he began to feel excessively tired. He had been working hard on a film, but no harder than usual. Even after he took a short vacation he still felt constantly fatigued. He was inclined to attribute the feeling to his age; after all, he was fifty-nine. A trip to a doctor revealed that he had an operable prostate condition, which is not uncommon in men of that age. Surgery in a Boston hospital seemed to take care of it. But five weeks later, in April, 1960, he had to undergo major intestinal surgery. He recovered, but the doctors urged him to submit to regular medical checkups.

Although the fatigued feeling persisted, Cooper agreed to make a film in London, *The Naked Edge*. By then he had lost a good deal of weight. Deborah Kerr and others who worked with him on the picture all felt that there was something terribly wrong. So did Rocky Cooper—and so, perhaps, did Cooper himself. Rather than worry his family and friends, he insisted on continuing the film until it was finished.

Back in Hollywood, he went to his personal physician for another series of checks. The doctors told him again that he should come back at stated intervals. They did not tell him what was actually wrong. Instead, they told Rocky.

Mrs. Cooper says, flatly, that what she remembers when she has to remember the last days is that it was on December 27, 1960, at 4:00 P.M., that she was asked to come to the doctor's office. She remembers that date, that time, as clearly as she remembers her birthday and her wedding anniversary; the whole grim calendar of days will remain with her as long as she lives. And so will the memory of the panic that possessed her as the doctor told her the awful news.

It was inoperable, he said. It was in both lungs.

"Now you'll have to enjoy *every day*," the doctor went on.

The doctor meant it well. He was her friend and her husband's. Today, when she thinks of that moment when she had the doctor's word, she speaks out of the reserve of strength, that almost super-human ability to get through that every human sometimes has to ask himself to produce, as she says, without a tinge of rancor:

"You know, it was too ridiculous. You couldn't enjoy any day. But you've got to try to make him enjoy it. And every day is one last day, and it's just horrible."

The doctors tried to be optimistic. One said, "Well . . . I've seen people live a year and a half, two years with this kind of thing."

She wanted to believe them; she could not believe them. She says: "Then, when Gary said to me—in February, middle of February, when he got back

178

from Utah, his hunting trip—when he said, 'Baby, what do I really have?' I'd go to the telephone, and I'd say to the doctor, 'I think we have to tell him.' Because he *knew*. You couldn't insult him by not telling. You can't lie to a person. He was no fool . . . and he was feeling, well, lousy. Plus the fact . . . well, maybe I still wouldn't have told him, but he wasn't taking care of himself, and we were afraid he'd get pneumonia. That would have done it . . .

"Gary always wore a bikini bathing suit around the yard, and he'd be out washing the car . . . in the shade, in the bikini suit. I could just see him getting pneumonia and going all at once."

She told him. "We told him," she says, referring to herself and her daughter.

"He did not bat an eye," she says.

She remembers the date that she told him, as she remembers all the dates. It was February 27, 1961, and they were getting ready to go to Florida.

He said, "I'm so glad that you let me know." His voice was heavy with tenderness for her, and with embarrassment for making her suffer on his account. And perhaps there was some relief in the sentence he uttered, for his secret suspense was over. Whatever it was that he felt, he in some way found strength to make things appear normal to his wife and daughter. Before they went home, he went to New York to do the narration for a documentary about the West that a television network previously had asked him to do. He must have been in a state of agony. None of his co-workers at the network knew.

"He would work a few hours," says his daughter, "and go back to the hotel and lie down."

"And take oxygen," his wife adds.

All three of them knew, when they got back to the house, that it would not be long. He went to bed and never really got up.

"In the beginning, he would appear for meals, take a little walk, and go right back to bed. Every week, it slows you down a little more," Mrs. Cooper says. "He was never under heavy sedation, not until the last five or six days. The pain comes through it anyway, you see. And what made it worse was that he had—as they said it in Sinatra's picture *Ocean's 11*— 'the big casino.' Bone. That's the most painful.

"I remember him talking one night with a priest here. And he said to him, 'I can certainly see now why there are times when people welcome death . . .' And oh! did his religion stand him in good stead! Every time he'd receive Holy Communion, he said he felt so much better. He was completely unafraid of the future. He really was. No fear whatsoever . . ."

Her voice trails off. A visitor ventures to ask, "How did you get through?"

She thinks. "You mean, to get in a frame of mind where you can accept it? Well, that's hard to say. Read books. The only thing that helps people—and don't forget, this thing hits one in three families—is their religion. And God help them if they don't have any. They go to pieces. Monsignor Dan Sullivan, of the Church of the Good Shepherd in Beverly Hills, was with the three of us a good deal. Oh, and Gary was made so happy by that special message he got from His Holiness, a cable . . . and then, on the night of the Rosary, Maria and I got one.

"*Peace of Soul*, by Bishop Fulton J. Sheen, did a great deal for me . . . and another one, *Seeds of Contemplation*, by Thomas Merton. Those books really helped . . ."

Forcibly, she pulls herself in hand and goes on, "We could talk to him all the time, except for the last two days. Then they really put him out, thank God."

"He never lost his sense of humor," the daughter says. "If anything, it got sharper toward the end."

Mrs. Cooper draws a breath, and returns to the last days. "Suffering brings you much closer to God. You can't say, 'I'll think about this tomorrow.' You can't escape it. You can go to sleep at night, that's not hard, but when you wake up in the morning, or in the middle of the night . . . and then you've had it. You start to think. Think, think, think . . . and only your faith can get you through that. If there was one thing I learned, it was that you've *got* to have a faith. . . . It was Gary's faith that made him brave, I'm certain of that."

The visitor asks if she will show him her husband's room.

"You can see it, but it's not the way it was when he was in it. I'm having it plastered over, redone completely. It's going to be a guest room. He certainly would approve of that, I know. And he would want us to stay on here. We're going to travel, Maria and I, visit friends. We're not going to sit around feeling sorry for ourselves. Other people have had worse things, as I said. Gary would want us to face life the way he did . . . and that's what we're going to do." She smiles and shrugs, as though to shake off her grief, to brush aside protestations of sympathy. "I mean, what else can we do but go on?"

And so Rocky Cooper and her daughter, Maria, go on living their lives—as the rest of us do, as the world does—and all of us, it perhaps is not too much to say, are a little better off for having known the brief presence of Gary Cooper, the tall American.

AUTHOR'S NOTE

John J. O'Connell, editor of *The American Weekly*, suggested in the summer of 1961 that I attempt to get an interview with Mrs. Gary Cooper and her daughter, Maria, in order to write an article about the last days of this notable, remarkable human being, and through the kindness of John Foreman, a family friend, I was enabled to do that. After the *Weekly* article appeared, it was reprinted in *Catholic Digest*, one of whose editors, Kay Sullivan, proposed that I do a full-length book for young people. I hesitated until I began observing the reading habits of my son, Scott, sixteen-going-on-seventeen, and discovered that they were not much different from my own. I went ahead, and I thank O'Connell, Kay Sullivan, Mrs. Cooper and Maria, John Foreman, and Scott. I also thank the mother, Mrs. Alice Cooper, who graciously consented to be interviewed about her son's early days.

The late Jerry Wald, the prolific producer, and his wife, Constance, also must be thanked. Mrs. Wald was having lunch one day with Maria Cooper and asked her, to my joy, if the latter and her mother would consent to be interviewed. John Foreman then set up an introduction. Wald himself proposed the title of the book. I am grateful to the Walds not only for these mechanical contributions but for a valuable and long-standing friendship.

In the course of the writing of this semi-fictional biography I talked to many people who knew Gary Cooper, and should like to mention the names of James

Stewart, John Wayne, Billy Wilder, Robert Mitchum, and Joe Hyams for their observations; I am in their debt. To add to my understanding, I read newspaper columns and magazine articles by George Scullin, Louella O. Parsons, Leonard Slater, Stan Optowsky, John Pascal, Hedda Hopper, Thomas B. Morgan, Leonard Lyons and the aforementioned Hyams. I thank them, and I thank Fred Narciso for digging this material out of morgues and back-date magazine shops. (I do not thank Narciso's penmanship teacher, who handicapped him for life.) Finally, I thank my wife, Betsy, for the patience she always summons when I am in the process of a long job, for her belief in my ability to finish it, and for her superior editorial judgment.

RG

INDEX

THE AUTHOR AND HIS BOOK

RICHARD GEHMAN, *forty, is a frequent contributor to magazines and the author of twelve books. He commutes between Hollywood and his home in Carmel, New York, and travels each year in Europe and Asia. During the past five years he has made annual trips around the world. He has taught in writers' courses at Bread Loaf, Indiana University, New York University and Columbia University, and is the author of a book on magazine article writing. He is married to the former Betsy Holland, herself a writer. They have two children, Pleasant Ann, four, and Charles Richard, two.*

THE TALL AMERICAN *(Hawthorn, 1963) was designed by Stefan Salter and completely manufactured by American Book–Stratford Press, Inc. The body type is Linotype Janson, based on the letters of Anton Janson, a Dutch punchcutter who worked between 1660 and 1687.*

A HAWTHORN BOOK

ABOUT CREDO BOOKS

CREDO BOOKS is an important new series of biographies that will appeal to both boys and girls. The subjects of these biographies are Catholic, but their stories are not of their faith so much as how that faith helped them to lead remarkable lives. Past and present will be represented here: a sculptor who left a priceless treasure of art to mankind, or a baseball player who has become an idol to young fans the world over; a movie star who was an idol of a different kind to young and old alike; the president of a South American country who fought against and lost his life to Communist terrorists. Heroes are made by the greatness of the human spirit and all the figures to be portrayed in CREDO BOOKS were great in spirit, courage and effort, no matter what task they took upon themselves.

The authors of these new books have been carefully chosen both for their ability to make biography come alive for young people and their knowledge of their subjects. Such authors as Hugh Ross Williamson, Lon Tinkle, Donald Demarest, Eva K. Betz, Ruth Hume, Frank Kolars and Jack Steffan will be represented.

To give CREDO BOOKS the benefit of their knowledge and experience, an editorial board of distinguished representatives from the fields of education, librarianship and the Catholic press, as well as Hawthorn's own editorial staff, choose both subjects and author for each book in the series.

As an example of the variety of personalities in this new series, you will find the following figures portrayed.

Father Hugh O'Flaherty, by Daniel Madden
Francis X. Ford, by Eva K. Betz
Paderewski, by Ruth and Paul Hume
Thomas More, by Margaret Stanley-Wrench
Joyce Kilmer, by Norah Smaridge
Gregor Mendel, by Gary Webster
Michelangelo, by Anne M. Peck with Frank and Dorothy
    Getlein
Col. Carlos Castillo Armas, by Jack Steffan
Ramon Magsaysay, by Gen. Carlos Romulo and Marvin
    Gray
Mother Katharine Drexel, by Katherine Burton
Tom Dooley, by Terry Morris
Juan Diego, by Lon Tinkle
Mary, Queen of Scots, by Hugh Ross Williamson
Fray Junipero Serra, by Donald Demarest
Charlemagne, by Col. T. N. Dupuy
Pedro Menendez, by Frank Kolars
Genevieve Caulfield, by Elizabeth Young
John McCormack, by Ruth and Paul Hume
Samuel de Champlain, by Charles Morrow Wilson
Louis Braille, by Webb Garrison
Gabriel Richard, by David Abodaher

There is adventure, suspense, excitement and information in CREDO BOOKS.

CREDO
BOOKS